Purple Sparks

Poetry by Sexual Assault Survivors

A Fundraiser for youthSpark Voices

Edited by

Dr. Stephanie Y. Evans &

Dr. Sharnell D. Myles

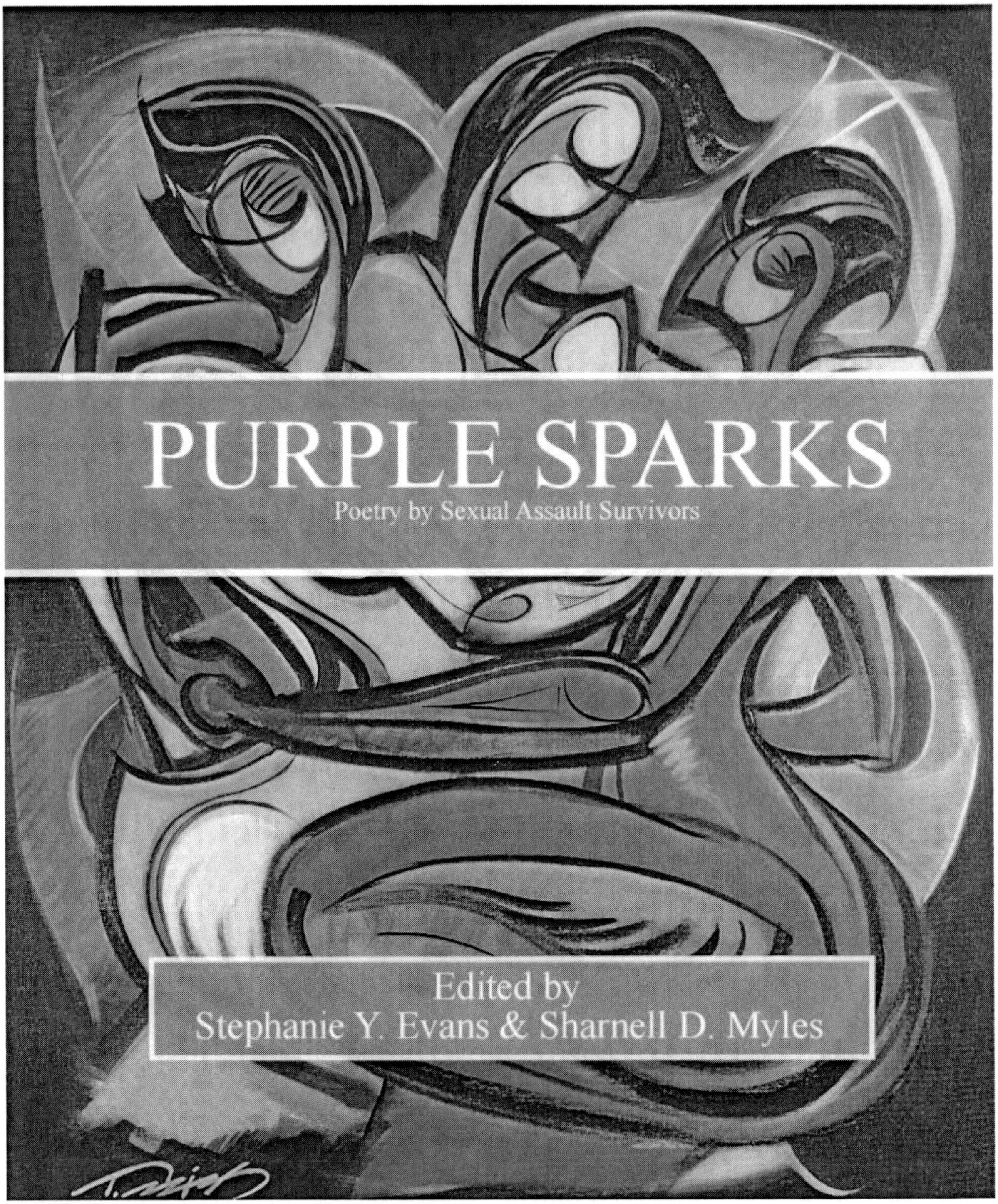

PURPLE SPARKS
Poetry by Sexual Assault Survivors

Edited by
Stephanie Y. Evans & Sharnell D. Myles

Purple Sparks:
Poetry by Sexual Assault Survivors

Published by youthSpark Voices, 2015
Atlanta, Georgia
http://www.youth-spark.org/

Purple Sparks © youthSpark Voices, 2015
Individual poems and art © contributors
Editor Introduction © Stephanie Y. Evans
Co-Editor Introduction © Sharnell D. Myles
Voices of Violet Cover Art © Tariq Mix, 2015

All rights reserved. No part of this publication may be reproduced, stored in a retrieval system, printed, distributed, or transmitted in any form or by any means without the written permission of the publisher.

All profits from this anthology will go to youthSpark Voices in Atlanta, Ga.

Purple Sparks:
Poetry by Sexual Assault Survivors

Purple Sparks is a collection of poetry and art; the publisher is not attempting to make any factual claims regarding the content provided by contributing authors. The views and content expressed in this work are solely those of the author and do not necessarily reflect the views of the publisher, therefore the publisher hereby disclaims any responsibility held by authors.

Full names and specific identifying details have been withheld to protect the privacy of individuals.

Dedication

To Arnesha Bowers,
RIP 2015
We are fighting for your freedom too....
and
To all survivors who have been shamed or not believed. To all survivors who have been victimized twice by doubt or the misplaced judgment of willfully ignorant bystanders.
SYE

To my parents Joyce and Jerry Frink:
Thank you for teaching me the power of love and laying the foundation to walk in my destiny.
and
To my Voices girls:
You have found your VOICE, now shout about it!
SDM

Special Thanks

The editors wish to extend a heartfelt thank you to the
Rape, Abuse, and Incest National Network (RAINN)
for encouraging Speakers Bureau members to submit poetry to *Purple Sparks*.
https://rainn.org/

Dr. Sharnell Myles, President Jimmy Carter, and Dr. Stephanie Evans
A Call to Action book signing and human trafficking discussion
Clark Atlanta University, February 13, 2015

Table of Contents

About youthSpark Voices	History, Mission, Vision, and Project Purpose	7
Preface	*Standing Together*, Jennifer Swain, youthSpark Deputy Director	8
Editor Introduction	*A Chorus of Purple Pens*, Stephanie Y. Evans	9
Editor Introduction	*The Audacity*, Sharnell Myles	21
Poems	Contributors	23
Voices	youthSpark Voices poems	117
Resources	Local and National Resource List	118
Bibliography	Suggested Reading	119
About the Editors	Evans, Myles, and Swain Bios	127

About youthSpark Voices

youthSpark is a 501 c3 organization based at the Fulton County Juvenile Court in Atlanta, Georgia serving exploited, abused, and neglected youth locally and providing resources nationwide. In 2010, youthSpark Voices was created, the first of its kind direct service prevention program in the nation, to work with young girls deemed "high risk" for child sex trafficking involvement. Uniquely designed to support and empower these girls, we partner directly with the Fulton County Juvenile Court and its Probation Department. As we are based at the Juvenile Court, we can reach our girls more effectively.

youthSpark's mission is to advocate for children that lack legal and adult protection in abusive and exploitative situations. Our vision is a world where no girl or boy is a product that can be bought, sold, or abused.

"Yesterday I Found My Voice, Today I'm Here To Shout About It!" is the affirmation of the program and our holistic, innovative approach, including a Child Sex Trafficking 101 curriculum, is a powerful agent for change. We look forward to the next steps of offering a replication process for youthSpark Voices in other jurisdictions.

Purple Sparks: Poetry by Sexual Assault Survivors offers a creative toolkit for healing and justice. This anthology shares poems from diverse populations—spanning age, gender, sexuality, race, nationality, religion, and experience. Our collection illuminates the broad scope of sexual violence and draws together a wide group of survivors into a fierce chorus.

Shame too often silences the abused and shields the guilty or powerful. In *Purple Sparks* we reclaim our voices by firing up our pens. We "talk back" to individual, social, cultural, and institutional perpetrators in order to ignite change.

Purple Sparks is very important to the girls we serve in youthSpark Voices, and our intervention program working with youth deemed high-risk for trafficking involvement, because many of them have experienced some form of child or sexual abuse and this anthology provides a different form of empowerment and healing. In addition to having their piece published in the book, proceeds from this project directly support the program's daily operations.

Authors in the *Purple Sparks* poetry anthology retain rights to their work, but have donated their poems to benefit the organization: 100% of book sales go to youthSpark VOICES.

To support the program, visit www.youth-spark.org.

spark voices!

spark pens!

spark awareness!

spark justice!

Preface

Standing Together

Jennifer Swain
Deputy Director, youthSpark

On difficult days I try to remind myself that serving society's most vulnerable youth—those who have been victimized by abuse, exploitation, and neglect—is an inherently difficult task for any organization or individual, but that it pales in comparison to the difficulty of surviving abuse. We at youthSpark understand the hurt, shame, and fear experienced by victims of sexual violence. These experiences can be extremely difficult to navigate and overcome, especially by young people. Through our work with *youthSpark Voices*, we witness firsthand the short- and long-term effects of sexual abuse, and we know how it leaves scars that last a lifetime.

How do we as a community create a world where hurt is replaced with healing, shame with pride, and fear with confidence? *Purple Sparks* seeks to peel back the intricate layers of hurt, shame, and fear; of healing, pride, and confidence associated with recovery from sexual violence. It takes an in-depth look at the personal journeys of those who endured tragedy, and how they use their voices to touch others.

This is not your typical anthology with submissions from typical poets. While their experiences with abuse are atypical, as individuals they are just like you and me: daughters, sons, parents, professionals, artists, teachers, and so on. Each piece was written to address rape, molestation, exploitation, or another form of sexual violence; their experiences impacted them forever, and connect them to one another. These poems may break your heart, but that is not the intention. These poets are trying to break the silence.

Each submission was written to empower others who know the feeling of abuse to step out of the darkness and into the light. To every poet whose discomfort is spread out on the following pages, THANK YOU. Thank you on behalf of each person who, after reading this anthology, feels strongly enough to tell or share their own journey. Thank you on behalf of each family that is able to come closer together again after having been torn apart by abuse. And especially thank you on behalf every little girl and boy who will be spared from silence and stigma because they now know they can live a life of happiness and purpose.

I would like to acknowledge Dr. Stephanie Evans and *Purple Pens* for her leadership of this project and believing in the power of prevention. Without her vision, this would not have been possible. I also want to acknowledge the work of the *Purple Sparks* Editorial Board, which provided thoughtful oversight for every submission. To the *youthSpark Voices* girls who contributed their work, thank you for leading the way on teen advocacy. To the readers of this collection, thank you for taking these stories into your heart—proceeds from the sale of this anthology directly support services for those who today are walking the same journeys as these poets. This is just one small way we can all stand together, no matter our path in life, to support those affected by sexual violence.

Editor Introduction

A Chorus of Purple Pens
Human Rights, Creative Recovery, and Collective Empowerment

Stephanie Y. Evans, PhD
Professor, Clark Atlanta University

This book is a meditation on freedom. We are survivors freeing ourselves from shame and joining together to eradicate the normalization of sexual violence. *Purple Sparks* is a creative, collective, and critical effort to advance human rights in theory and practice. Contributors to this anthology share intimately human stories. These poems contribute the best humanity has to offer, despite the worst of circumstances.

Contributors come from a variety of racial, ethnic, gender, sexuality, geographic, religious and experiential backgrounds. Our writing reveals a spectrum of realities: memory, forgetting, silence, voice, premature death, survival, victory, solace, breaking, healing, forgiveness, damnation, criminality, post-traumatic stress (PTSD), and reflection. There are bodies weirdly strewn, cruel pianos, crushed velvet, angry hippies, and children forced to cross borders of pain no one should have to even imagine. There is dissemblance and reclamation. Yes, there is unloving here. But these poems elicit compassion more than vengeance; they demand justice more than pity. At the very least, this gathering of over 50 narrators encourage solidarity against the social stigma of shaming victims who dare not only to survive, but who have the courage to demand justice for themselves and for others.

Research and resources accompany poetry to assist in a deeper understanding of the locations, circumstances, and arenas of abuse. These resources also extend our capacity to form effective and sustainable strategies to prevent or heal from violence. Following the collection of poems, a bibliography of books, dissertations, and journal articles are offered to give context to the voices provided through creative expression. The resource bibliography is designed to raise awareness for prevention, but also to offer valuable information to millions of survivors who are still struggling to find their voice.

The resource list, like our poems will serve professionals who are committed to helping survivors thrive through an exploration of the lived experience and the sociological, psychological, historical, and political dimensions of sexual violence. Most significantly, the voices and stories provided in this collection bind together those who may have mistakenly believed they were at fault for their own abuse or that they were alone in their struggle to reclaim their lives after having survived. As youthSpark Deputy Director Jennifer Swain indicated in her preface, we stand together and in this reflective reading of our lives, we stand strong to not only face our past but to positively impact humanity in the future.

RECOVERING FROM CRUELTY AND DEGRADATION

While the UN Universal Declaration of Human Rights (UDHR) does not specifically mention sexual violence, the document's language helps us better understand that rape, molestation, domestic abuse, female genital mutilation, sexual harassment, trafficking, and other forms of violence are human rights issues. We are all endowed with rights to security of person and protection from cruel, inhuman, or degrading treatment.

Articles 1-5 of the United Nations Universal Declaration of Human Rights[1] articulate every person's right of self-possession and freedom from violence:

---

[1] UN Universal Declaration of Human Rights http://www.un.org/en/documents/udhr/

- Article 1. All human beings are born free and equal in dignity and rights. They are endowed with reason and conscience and should act towards one another in a spirit of brotherhood.
- Article 2. Everyone is entitled to all the rights and freedoms set forth in this Declaration, without distinction of any kind, such as race, colour, sex, language, religion, political or other opinion, national or social origin, property, birth or other status. ...
- Article 3. Everyone has the right to life, liberty and security of person.
- Article 4. No one shall be held in slavery or servitude; slavery and the slave trade shall be prohibited in all their forms.
- Article 5. No one shall be subjected to torture or to cruel, inhuman or degrading treatment or punishment.

Further, the UN Convention of the Rights of the Child[2], adopted in 1989 recognized the need to include specific language about sexual violence:

- Article 19. 1. States Parties shall take all appropriate legislative, administrative, social and educational measures to protect the child from all forms of physical or mental violence, injury or abuse, neglect or negligent treatment, maltreatment or exploitation, including sexual abuse, while in the care of parent(s), legal guardian(s) or any other person who has the care of the child.
- Article 34. States Parties undertake to protect the child from all forms of sexual exploitation and sexual abuse. For these purposes, States Parties shall in particular take all appropriate national, bilateral and multilateral measures to prevent: (a) The inducement or coercion of a child to engage in any unlawful sexual activity; (b) The exploitative use of children in prostitution or other unlawful sexual practices; (c) The exploitative use of children in pornographic performances and materials.

Historical context is essential in assessing and addressing the issue and taking time to learn and teach human rights is an essential step in better assisting those recovering from abuse. Too many have internalized abuse as their fault rather than conceiving it as a broad social issue with deep political, cultural, and geographic dimensions. History is instructive to help contextualize, interpret and more effectively prevent sexual cruelty, yet understanding of these issues must go beyond historical study of time and place: psychological services are essential for healing in the here and now and preventing perpetuation of violent traditions.

Thema Bryant-Davis, a leading scholar-activist on the issue of sexual violence, is associate professor of psychology at Pepperdine University and former President of the Society for the Psychology of Women. She has served as an American Psychological Association representative to the United Nations and in her practical guide, *Surviving Sexual Violence: A Guide to Recovery and Empowerment*, she writes,

> Sexual assault is so much more than the event itself. The person is left with feelings of helplessness, powerlessness, self-blame, and shame. Bad choices after the event create more feelings of self-loathing. Post-traumatic stress untreated can last for a lifetime, leaving the victims with chronic symptoms and loss of potential for a happy life.[3]

We are committed to securing the opportunity for a happy life for ourselves and others. The Daniel Holtzclaw and Jared Fogel cases exposed that "good guys" are sometimes the most heinous predators. Social attitudes toward sexual violence (compounded by the expansion of social media) largely blame victims and those "innocent until proven guilty" are often perpetrators who are never proven guilty—in a court of law or otherwise. Hostility toward victims during all phases of the reporting and legal process which contributes to relatively low level of reporting and prosecution of

---

[2] UN Convention on the Rights of the Child http://www.ohchr.org/en/professionalinterest/pages/crc.aspx
[3] (2011-10-16). Surviving Sexual Violence: A Guide to Recovery and Empowerment (p. 135). Rowman & Littlefield Publishers. Kindle Edition.

perpetrators exacerbates the negative social stigma for survivors that speak up. Though there are periodic stories that pierce the silence, and several vital national and international movements have been formed by and for survivors, there is still an unsatisfactory tone around reporting, and there are too-few opportunities for survivors to join in coalition in order to fight *all types* of abuse and exploitation.

<u>Voice: Moving from Worthless to Astounding (Overcoming Shame)</u>
> **S:** "Choose one word that represents your past, one for your present, and one for your future."
> **K:** "The word for my past is worthless. I feel worthless because of what happened to me. The word for my future is astounding. I know I can do great things. I don't have a word for my present. How do I get from worthless to astounding?"
> ~ Purple Pens Poetry Workshop[4]

In Spring 2015, I developed Purple Pens Poetry Workshops for survivors of sexual violence in order to share words of encouragement and empowerment. As a survivor of several attacks during my childhood and young adulthood, I eventually found my voice through poetry and through making a career of studying African American women writers. By learning the healing traditions in Black women's intellectual history, I slowly developed an emotionally, socially, and professionally grounded life. I created workshops out of a desire to combat the social stigma surrounding survival and to help others along their paths of love and struggle.

As evidenced by Ray Rice, R. Kelly and Bill Cosby stories in 2014 and 2015, victims of sexual violence are often re-victimized in the media by public shaming campaigns that blame victims. The ongoing attention to the Cosby case, the vitriolic backlash to protect Cosby's reputation, and snail pace of acceptance of women's voices triggered many women who have struggled to find voice for healing and empowerment to act. In addition to holding public figures such as these accountable for their actions, it is also imperative that we unmask the face of abusers and recognize the pervasiveness in all communities—far beyond the convenient image of the Black male rapist trope. Demographics of abusers are as broad as victims and most prey on those closest to them so the celebrities are merely projections of the problems we have in our churches, schools, workplaces, and in our own homes. Those men who purchase adolescent girls (and increasingly boys) for sex in Georgia come from every age, ethnicity, and income bracket.

At the Purple Pens workshop for youthSpark's Voices group in April 2015, I brought several sample poems to share with a group of young women in the sex-trafficking intervention program—most of whom had experienced some form of abuse and neglect. I worked in concert with licensed counselors who collaborate to form a supportive scaffolding for healthy identity development—but on that day, I did not have an immediate or clear answer for K's question, "How do survivors of abuse get from worthless to astounding?" In hindsight, I would simply say to her: by defining your own power. Power of definition changes shame into triumph. Purple Pens workshops have four goals: eliminate *stigma* of being a survivor, share *testimony*, encourage *activism* around sexual violence and prevention, and provide *resources* (STAR purpose) http://www.purplepens.net/.

Purple is the color of royalty and survival; like the herb lavender or the Yoruba Orisha Nana Baruku, the color purple is a nurturer for those who have been violated. Themes in *Purple Sparks* shed light on innermost feelings of those who have experienced rape, molestation, female genital mutilation, sex trafficking, incest, domestic violence, and other forms of sexual violence. Readers will witness survivors turn to drugs for escape, rely on religion for salvation, create art as resistance, and survive out of sheer will, spite, and desperate desire for self-love. From all over the United States to Canada, Jamaica, and Australia, poets sound off to increase the volume of voices from youthSpark in Atlanta, Georgia.

---

[4] Purple Pens Poetry Workshop, April 30, 2015. Quote used with permission of youthSpark Voices.

CREATIVE TESTIMONY AND RECOVERY

Sexual violence is a pervasive but preventable global crisis. As seen worldwide, violence has substantial psychological impact on women's mental health (Punamäki, *Journal of Peace Research*).[5] The Center for Disease Control reports that at least 1 in 5 women—**ONE IN FIVE WOMEN**—in the United States are victimized by rape or sexual assault, and the *"No!" The Rape Documentary* by Adishah Simmons takes into account the severe underreporting and likelihood that 1 in 3 Black women experience sexual violence (CDC, 2011).[6] Ashley Callingbull, the only First Nations woman to win Ms. Universe is very vocal about her survival and adamant about her activism to raise awareness of the abuse, rape, and murder of Indigenous women in Canada and around the world.[7] Many have expressed discomfort at her candor, but her willingness to break the silence about her own experience is exactly what is needed to lift the veil off of the timeless tradition of killing women and children and using rape as a weapon of genocide or war, even in times when a national climate seems peaceful on the surface.

Despite efforts of organizations like V-Day, SAAM, and RAINN, 1 in 5 American women will be raped in our lifetime yet, given the prevalence of this epidemic, the level of shame that still surrounds being a survivor is astonishing. Shame feeds the silence that inhibits education, public dialogue, and prevention. Violence is often at the root of other far-reaching mental health issues, as can be seen in *Not All Black Girls Know How to Eat*, a memoir by Stephanie Armstrong where she identifies being raped by an uncle as the seed of her struggle with bulimia.[8]

Like countless activists engaged in struggle against sexual violence, the editors and contributors of *Purple Sparks: Poetry by Sexual Assault Survivors* refuse to concede that we must sit on our hands and accept the seemingly inevitable beating, battering, cutting, raping, or profit from our pain. We write to embrace creative, collective, and collaborative peace.[9]

In many ways, this collection of poetry comprises a group therapeutic effort, which Dr. Bryant-Davis acknowledges can effective:

> ...there is no "one way" victims [of sexual violence] react to such a devastating crime. While psychological symptoms vary during recovery, many victims experience guilt, shame, fear, embarrassment, tension, crying spells, anxiety, an exaggerated startle response, depression, anger (both generalized and directed toward men), discomfort in social situations, rapid mood swings, and/or impaired memory and concentration. Years later, survivors are more likely to have a serious psychiatric diagnosis such as major depression, drug abuse and dependence, generalized anxiety, post-traumatic stress disorder, and obsessive-compulsive disorder. ... Feminist therapeutic approaches...focus on longer-term symptoms like guilt, shame, and self-blame. They employ shared goal setting, the identification of rape as a social issue as opposed to a personal problem, and focus on gender

---

[5] Punamäki, R-L. Relationships between political violence and psychological responses among Palestinian women, p. 84.

[6] Simmons, http://notherapedocumentary.org/

[7] Ms. Universe on Canada's Missing and Murdered Indigenous Women. http://www.theglobeandmail.com/news/national/ashley-callingbull-on-canadas-missing-and-murdered-aboriginal-women/article26611740/. Accessed October 2, 1015.

[8] These and additional issues will be addressed in the forthcoming edited volume by Stephanie Y. Evans, Kanika Bell, and Nsenga Burton, *Black Women's Mental Health: Balancing Strength and Vulnerability* http://www.bwmentalhealth.net

[9] Poetry workshops are an outstanding opportunity to learn and grow, however, they are often more effective when facilitators pay attention to form and offer clear guidelines for construction. As an example, Professor Sonia Sanchez includes Haiku in her public talks and encourages her students to create their own form, as she did with "Sonku" (Sanchez, 2007). Similarly, Nick Mazza engaged the new and popular "six word memoir" in a mentoring group (Mazza, 2012).

inequities. Because feminist therapy places a focus on self-blame, guilt, and shame, group therapy is often preferred.[10]

The use of poetry for healing is as old as poetry itself, but formal poetry therapy is an invention of the twentieth century. Development is traced to the 1920s, but professionalization came decades later:

> [By the 1960s] mental health professionals were exploring the therapeutic value of literary materials, especially of poetry. Their contribution to the emerging discipline was two-fold: 1) they emphasized the evocative value of literature, particularly poetry because of its metaphor, imagery, rhythm and other poetic devices; and 2) they recognized the beneficial potential of having clients write their response to published literature or their original material, drawing on their own experiences and emotions." (*IFBPT Guide*, 7)

It is significant that poetry therapy has been identified as useful for practitioners of family therapy and work with survivors of domestic or sexual violence:

> Poetry, like drama and other arts, provides another perspective or way of approaching the truth. When the poet is also the victim, the perspective becomes even more compelling. Battered women's experiences, reactions, and methods of coping with abuse can be expressed through the language and imagery of poetry. Kissman (1989, p. 225) noted that there are numerous examples of women's poetry that show how creativity can be used as a survival mechanism: "Women who are isolated with their 'secrets' of battering, rape, and incest can tie into the collective and communal network of the written word which is rich in metaphors about women's experiences." The publication of poetry in women's shelter or program newsletters across the country is one example of how the network is being strengthened. (Mazza, 2013)

Poetry therapy is one kind of applied creative non-fiction, and a main branch of bibliotherapy which includes journals and memoirs, among other types of writing. Music therapy and broader forms of art therapy present additional opportunities for growth. Naturally, there are many areas where memoir, poetry, and music intersect. The most shining example is Maya Angelou, who traverses several genres and whose example offers a poignant example of the power of written word. Before becoming close friends with Angelou, Oprah Winfrey gained strength from the book *I Know Why the Caged Bird Sings*, and especially benefitted from Angelou's tale of surviving childhood rape. As evidenced by Winfrey, the concept of literary mentoring is effective: readers can be mentored by life stories in books similar to how they are mentored in person (Evans, *Black Passports*, 2014). Many learn that part of exercising self-preservation in order to provide encouragement for the next generation necessarily involves sharing our own testimony.

Praise the Day Suggarpuddin' Found Her Voice

Part of my childhood was very privileged: I saw much of the best things the world had to offer through precious moments with a caring family. I was fortunate to live abroad in Germany for three years from age seven to ten, which opened my eyes to the wonders of food, language, education, and culture outside of the United States. The other part of my childhood was filled with sexual violence in a trauma-laden extended "family," lack of parental awareness, sink-or-swim abandonment, negligence from caretakers (I moved out at 16 years old), recurring psychological terror from men of all ages (Black and White), repeated attacks from neighbors and family friends, incidents of domestic violence during my twenties, and a sinking feeling that the world held for me

---

[10] (2011-10-16). *Surviving Sexual Violence: A Guide to Recovery and Empowerment* (p. 119). Rowman & Littlefield Publishers. Kindle Edition.

only danger and pain. Reading movie star Pam Grier's explicit recollection of rape at age six and again in her college years stunned me because my attacks occurred at similar ages. But, I lived and live still. I had life-saving help in the form of a role model teacher in 8th grade and, when personal attention was lacking, I made books my salve.

I was attacked to varying degree by five different perpetrators when I was between the ages of 6 and 21.... By the time I was seven years old (pictured below in a passport photo), I had already been abused and threatened with death if I told. Predators target vulnerable populations and the shame of abuse silences the weak and shields the guilty or powerful. Silence is deadly, but victim education, mental health advocacy, and increased social awareness are essential parts of healing. Increasing critical and informed public dialogue can be a key factor in empowering victims to make meaning of their experience in ways that overcome self-blame, self-hate, and prevent continuing a cycle of violence. For example, the value of victim education can be seen by couching my story within several references in the bibliography that speak to directly to my experience. To better understand my abuse, one might read texts such as

- *Revictimization in women's lives: An empirical and theoretical account of the links between child sexual abuse and repeated sexual violence*. Haskell, Lori. University of Toronto (Canada), ProQuest Dissertations Publishing, 1999. 
- Conflict, Power, and Violence in Families. Kristin L. Anderson. *Journal of Marriage and Family*, Vol. 72, No. 3 (June 2010), pp. 726-742.
- *Asking for It: The Alarming Rise of Rape Culture--and What We Can Do about It*. 2015. Kate Harding
- *Preventing Sexual Violence: Interdisciplinary Approaches to Overcoming a Rape Culture*. 2014. Nicola Henry and Anastasia Powell
- *Rape, Incest, Battery: Women Writing Out the Pain*. 2000. Miriam Harris

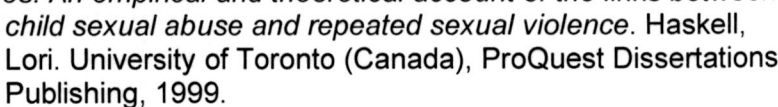

Early in my life, I was set on a path to violence. Abused at several turns, I sharpened my will for self-preservation, worked to break the chain of abuse, got mental health counseling to enrich my quality of life and, eventually, gained the strength to partner with others committed to the defiant act of loving ourselves. Through Black Studies, Women's Studies and Black women's intellectual history, I came to learn my worth as a human and as one in a long legacy of Black women survivors who became scholar-activists, including Katherine Dunham (with whom I have always felt close because we share the same birthday).

Through reading Black women's writing, I developed a healthy self-concept and recently reflected that, "A vital part of self-possession or owning the self is the ability to formulate a positive *self*-concept, especially in the midst of a negative environment that insists on your degradation and dehumanization. Dunham articulated that the first step in an empowerment curriculum was 'humanization,' and in her research, she articulated a phenomenon of 'self-examination' necessary for a student to actively engage in a process of intellectual agency. In the field of anthropology, Dunham pioneered international dance studies at the University of Chicago while conducting research in Haiti and several other Caribbean countries. ... For Dunham, travel abroad created a transnational identity grounded in a fight for human rights, a fight built on spiritual reflection, Black humanization, and a life of dancing one's culture" (Evans, *Black Passports*, 140-141). Survivors of racism, sexism, heterosexism, religious persecution, and sexual abuse are victims of dehumanization. Finding a way to love one's self is a radical and necessary act of re-humanization. Being able to sit with oneself, alone, in peace and love oneself—which I practice in my daily meditation—is truly an act of resistance.

Survivors are often met by family members, communities, media figures, or institutions that are willfully ignorant, indifferent, or hostile to what is perceived to be a women's issue concerned only with the morally weak or unremorsefully slutty. *But statistics show that, even if you weren't raped, your mother, grandmother, sister, cousin, auntie or someone in your family probably has been. The CDC cites 1 in 5 women and 1 in 59 men have been raped in their lifetime.* Sexual violence is EVERYONE'S concern. We <u>must</u> talk about it to keep it from happening to others.

My Gramms' nickname for me was Sugarpuddin' - it is for her, for all of the women in my family, for my students who have shared their stories over the past two decades, and for women around the world being tortured daily that I pick up my purple pen for **peace**...and encourage others to pick up theirs as well. We need to be part of a global justice movement...in coalition with other anti-violence movements. We can do this work in so many ways—in this anthology survivors join together by picking up or pens and raising our voices.

Writing empowers people to have a stronger efficacy in four areas: self, communication, tasks, and innovation. Poetry can strengthen survivors' voices, voices can strengthen advocate communities, and advocate communities can strengthen activism for change of culture and policy. At the very least, it can end the deafening silence and eliminate the culture of shame. At most, survivors' writing can silence abusive critics who dehumanize entire populations and our voices can shape our collective future to look drastically different than our miserable past.

I survived and I ain't shamed. Run tell dat.

***

In essence, poems represent three phases of experience as survivors: Past (Hurt), Present (Healing), Future (Hope). Adding my voice to the chorus, my poems are below.

The Past

<u>6, 11, 16, 19, 21</u>
Seems the whole world knows
Black girls are easy targets
Unlucky numbers

<u>Dirge for Skinny Black Bitches</u>
Funny how a rape
Alters food relationships
Some will gorge—some starve

<u>Hurt People Hurt People - Breaking the Cycle</u>
Early in my life
I had to choose not to die
Then choose not to kill

The Present

<u>Praise the Day That Sugarpuddin' Found Her Voice: My Love Song for the Underdog (A Drabble)*</u>
When I was six years old I made a decision to save my own life. Facing the threat of drowning by an abuser if I "told," I claimed my voice to yell my truth--come what may, death be damned--because I was determined not to die unheard. And I have not stopped shouting since. Underdog liberation depends on "self-care, self-respect, self-reliance, and fearlessness." But freedom is also collective…. My life is a praise song to Ancestors who helped me find Grace when all seemed lost. My song is an ode to those who fear nothing…not even their own power.
*Drabble: a short story of exactly 100 words

<u>No Shame in Survival</u>
I won't be silent
Victims' shame shields the guilty
Pride is resistance

<u>Unbroken</u>
Some say success is
the best revenge…It is not
my revenge is JOY.

The Future

Toward Joy
Misery is not my
inheritance
Every being has a right to
grow
So I bend my energy

Toward joy

Breathing peace in all things
Work, justice, survival, play and
serious fun
Moving life backward, inward,
forward

Toward joy

Ancestors hear my living plea
Help me shape these words for
them
Who be, know, do struggle

Toward joy

Poetry helped me find my voice in 1994 when I began college at the age of twenty-five. I published a book of poetry titled *What Lies Inside* as a means to raise money for tuition; much of the poetry chronicled my survival of violence and bookmarked my entry into college as a new era of me developing my own power. Twenty years later, it now makes sense for me to return to poetry as a tool of human rights education, community empowerment, and a means to provide bibliotherapy resources informed by both my experience and my research.

New stories are reported regularly, including rapes involving military, border patrol, police, and corrections officers, sports teams, college campuses, and increasingly school girls--from the #BringBackOurGirls movement in Nigeria to a first year student at Owen Labrie and New England Prep school. And then there are the boys. As Antwone Fisher wrote as a male survivor of a female rape, "who will cry for the boys?!" We will cry and fight. And for those who are gay, lesbian, transgender, intersex and those who have yet to be born. We will cry and fight for those who have had one brush with abuse and especially for those who are pimped out as children so they may be conditioned to be pimped out as adults. Because sex trafficking and commercial sexual exploitation of children (CSEC) continues to be underreported and under-prosecuted. We have much work yet to do.[11]

COLLECTIVE EMPOWERMENT

As a trafficking awareness and prevention agency in Atlanta, youthSpark works to educate the public about human rights violations in our own back yard and working with youth at-risk or who are survivors of trafficking. There are too many victims of this PREVENTABLE criminal activity:

> "The numbers are staggering — 12,400 men each month in Georgia pay for sex with a young female, 7,200 of whom end up exploiting an adolescent female. These men account for 8,700 paid sex acts with adolescent females each month, which means that each adolescent female is exploited an average of 3 times per night." *Men Who Buy Sex with Adolescent Girls: A Scientific Research Study.* February, 2010.[12]

Women's quest for peace and justice are too often made invisible, trivialized, or misrepresented. This collection presents a rainbow of diverse people who stand in solidarity with those victimized in Atlanta and around the world.

As the majority of girls in the youthSpark Voices program are African American, historic research provides useful context. Sexual violence is traumatic; in a hostile social environment that not only blames and shames victims, but deems Black women "unrapable," the trauma is increased (Lenhart, 2006). In the African diaspora, Black women have penned life stories that offer insight into the shifting kaleidoscope of violence and harrowing social experiences with domestic and

---

[11] Systematic sexual violence by U.S. State agencies: A victimology approach. Brightman, Sarah. Western Michigan University, ProQuest Dissertations Publishing, 2011. NPR, Prep School Rape Trial Puts Spotlight On High School Assaults. http://www.npr.org/2015/08/29/435741103/prep-school-rape-trial-puts-spotlight-on-high-school-assaults

[12] Report online http://www.youth-spark.org/learn/trafficking-resource-hub/.

sexual violence, foster care or forced child home systems, public humiliation, inadequate health care, employment discrimination, and disenfranchisement that have negatively impacted their physical and mental health. Available narratives include:

Stories of Rape, Molestation, Assault, Domestic Abuse, Harassment, and FGM in Memoirs

1. Laila Ali, *Reach!: Finding Strength, Spirit and Personal Power*
2. Maya Angelou, *I Know Why the Caged Bird Sings*
3. Asha Bandele, *The Prisoner's Wife*
4. Violet Barungi, *Farming Ashes: Tales of Agony and Resilience*
5. Halima Bashir, *Tears of the Desert: A Memoir of Survival in Dafur*
6. Angela Bassett, *Friends: A Love Story*
7. Donna Britt, *Brothers (and Me): A Memoir of Loving and Giving*
8. Betty Brown, *Open Secrets: A Poor Person's Life in Higher Education*
9. Cupcake Brown, *Piece of Cake: A Memoir*
10. Julian Bullock, *Here I Stand*
11. Ayana Byrd, *Naked: Black Women Bare All About Their Skin, Hair, Lips, and Other Parts*
12. Theresa Cameron, *Foster Care Odyssey: A Black Girl's Story*
13. Shanetris Campbell, *I Am Not My Father's Daughter*
14. Diahann Carroll, *The Legs Are the Last to Go*
15. Vera Chapelle, *Beauty and Truth: Journeying through Joy and Sorrow, Pain and Peace*
16. Letty Chihoro, *Loving Me: Reclaiming my Power*
17. Julia Jeter Cleckley, *A Promise Fulfilled: My Life as a Wife and Mother Soldier and General Officer*
18. Iris Cooke, *The Little Black Book of Child Sex Slavery*
19. Cynthia Cooper, *She Got Game: My Personal Odyssey*
20. Dorothy Cotton, *If Your Back's Not Bent: The Role of the Citizenship Education Program in the Civil Rights Movement*
21. Stephanie Covington Armstrong, *Not All Black Girls Know How to Eat*
22. Lorie Crawford, *Memoirs of a Black Woman: The Tale of Two Women*
23. Delores Cross: *Beyond the Wall*
24. Sandra Pepa Denton, *Let's Talk About Pep*
25. Debra Dickerson, *An American Story*
26. Waris Dirie, *Desert Flower*
27. Patricia Due, *Freedom in the Family: A Mother Daughter Memoir of the Fight for Civil Rights*
28. Katherine Dunham, *Loss of Innocence*
29. Stacie Farr, *Black Girl in America*
30. Patrice Gaines, *Laughing in the Dark: From Colored Girl to Woman of Color*
31. Robin Givens, *Grace Will Lead Me Home*
32. Marita Golden, *Migrations of the Heart*
33. Pam Grier, *Foxy: My Life in Three Acts*
34. Marilynn Griffith, *SistahFaith: Real Stories of Pain, Truth and Triumph*
35. Saidiya Hartman, *Lose Your Mother: A Journey Along the Atlantic Slave Route*
36. Martha Hawkins, *Finding Martha's Place: My Journey Through Sin, Salvation, and Lots of Soul Food*
37. Ruth Hegerty, *Bittersweet Journey*
38. Anita Hill, *Speaking Truth to Power*
39. Endesha Ida Mae Holland, *From the Mississippi Delta*
40. Billie Holliday, *Lady Sings the Blues*
41. Kate Howarth, *Ten Hail Marys*
42. Edith Hudley, *Raise Up a Child: Human Development in an African American Family*
43. Harriet Jacobs, *Incidents in the Life of a Slave Girl, Written by Herself Linda Brent*
44. Ellen Johnson-Sirleaf, *This Child Will be Great*
45. Queen Latifah, *Put on Your Crown: Life-Changing Moments on the Path to Queendom*
46. Soraya Mire, *The Girl with Three Legs*
47. Ilyasa Shabazz, *Growing Up X*
48. Assata Shakur, *Assata*
49. Nina Simone, *I Put a Spell on You*
50. Alice Swafford, *Conquering the Darkness*
51. Tina Turner, *I Tina!*
52. Essie Mae Washington-Williams, *Dear Senator: A Memoir by the Daughter of Strom Thurmond*
53. Ethel Waters, *His Eye is on the Sparrow*
54. Ida B. Wells-Barnett, *Crusade for Justice*
55. Malinda West, *Black Gal: Sharecropper's Daughter Triumphant Journey Out of Poverty*
56. Mary Williams, *The Lost Daughter*
57. Wendy Williams, *Wendy's Got the Heat*
58. Jan Willis, *Dreaming Me: Black Baptist and Buddhist*
59. Mary Wilson, *Dreamgirl and Supreme Faith*
60. Shakeeta Winfrey, *The Other Winfrey*
61. Kaye Wright, *Messy Marvin: A Story of Abuse and Survival*

Men's Stories
62. Antwone Fisher, *Finding Fish: Antwone Fisher*
63. Carlos Santana, *The Universal Stone: Bringing My Story to Light*

In addition, racial protectionism, ethnic allegiances, and familial loyalties exacerbate institutional and public violence. Thus, triggers for survivors of color are everywhere and culturally relevant approaches are imperative. Yet, as this collection demonstrates, stories from numerous marginalized perspectives must be reclaimed. Each perspective can offer additional information useful for those trying to heal from specific types of wounds. The mosaic of differently-shaped narratives creates a quilt of broad and deep texture to help us to better understand the unifying factors of survival.

Living free from torture, enslavement, or degradation is a human right. This collection moves us closer to recognizing this as a universal imperative.

Conclusion: A Tradition of Creative Human Rights

> Rights contain images of power, and manipulating those images, either visually or linguistically, is central in the making and maintenance of rights. In principle, therefore, the more dizzyingly diverse the images that are propagated, the more empowered we will be as a society. ~ Patricia J. Williams (1991)

> *This RIGHT TO GROW is sacred and inviolable, based on the solidarity and undeniable value of humanity itself and linked with the universal value and inalienable rights of all individuals.* ~ Anna Julia Cooper (1925)[13]

The reflections in *Purple Sparks* poems challenge power that has traditionally been defined in terms of domination. By submitting work for inclusion in this anthology, these authors refuse to submit to personal, social, and structural violence. Their rejection of violence helps foster healthy and balanced mental, emotional, and intellectual development. We are not alone, we are in good company.

Just as there are many examples of trauma narratives, there are also historical empower narratives. For example, Anna Julia Heyward Cooper is a historical figure that can provide vital encouragement for current survivors. Cooper was born enslaved... the product of a rape—her father was presumably her mother's "owner" who was "lent" out after having two children (Cooper's older brothers) by her former owner. Like many survivors, Cooper wrote that her mother Hannah Stanley Haywood, bore the shame of violence; however, Cooper also acknowledged that her mother not only survived bearing three children by rapist slave owners, but that she claimed a long and happy life after emancipation, despite her early life of pain, degradation, and suffering. Cooper wrote,

> "My mother was a slave and the finest woman I have ever known.... Presumably my father was her master; if so I owe him not a sou and she was always too modest and shamefaced to ever mention him" (emphasis added).[14]

With unique experiential insight, Anna Julia Cooper used higher education to advance human rights in theory and practice. She built her life's work of scholar-activism on the desire to educate and advocate for those most neglected and abused. She was born in Raleigh, North Carolina in 1858 and lived to the age of 105--and earned her doctorate at the age of 66. Dr. Cooper advocated for "the rights of all" a half century before the 1948 United Nations Universal Declaration of Human Rights. Just as Ghandi and Martin Luther King Jr. are recognized as drum majors for civil rights, Cooper's social justice work is a paradigm for human rights in general and survivors in particular. Growth is a right, but also the responsibility of everyone in a society. Dr. Cooper argued that ALL human beings have a right to grow...and she demonstrated the tradition of creative growth by

---

[13] Anna Julia Cooper in speech delivered in 1925 at Howard University, published in 1945. "The Third Step." In *The voice of Anna Julia Cooper*. New York: Rowman & Littlefield.
[14] *The Voice of Anna Julia Cooper*, p. 331.

penning several poems of her own. The poems in this anthology provide examples of how beautiful and fulfilling personal growth after tragedy can be. Yet authors also make clear the shame is no longer ours to carry…we now lay that burden down at the feet of those responsible for perpetuating violence.

***

Taken together, the collection of poetry is an act of self-preservation and unwillingness to accept the continuation of unchecked aggression of <u>any</u> contact without consent.[15]
This poetry anthology builds on artistic activist work of projects like *Furies: A Poetry Anthology of Women Warriors* (2014) which benefitted rape crisis centers in England and Wales, but *Purple Sparks* is unique in several ways. As a collective,
- we connect various types of sexual violence and include widely diverse survivor voices
- we reflect an organic academic/non-profit agency relationship useful to create sustainable community building practice and solid community engagement partnerships
- we are both deconstructive (project seeks to eliminate survivor shame) and constructive (supports child sex-trafficking intervention and prevention program)
- we provide connection to assistance hotlines, national advocacy groups, and bibliographic research to encourage study and to assist training more effective activists and practitioners.

Partnering with youthSpark for a community-based research course on scholar-activist Anna Julia Cooper, Dr. Myles and the youthSpark team also provided additional keywords to advance understanding of survivor experiences. These concepts included trust, maternal history of sexual abuse, shame, communication, hopelessness, and learned helplessness.

Those of us engaging in this discourse join other voices to raise awareness about issues such as out-of-control gun violence, unmitigated and disproportionate incarceration rates, police brutality, feminization of poverty, and global dislocation of refugees of war. It is not enough to confront public locales of violence, we must also address the uncomfortable topic of private spaces where intimate violence occurs; those who fight against violence in the streets must join us in our fight against violence in the sheets. As survivors of "torture, cruelty, and degradation," we have much to say about the violence we have endured and the imperative to address human rights abuses in all spaces. Violence is a problem; as Dr. Cooper argued, "adding our voice to the chorus," contributing our artistic reflections, and learning from our experience is part of the solution.[16]

Works Cited

Angelou, M. (1969). *I know why the caged bird sings*. New York: Random House. In *The collected autobiographies of Maya Angelou* (Modern Library, 2012).
Armstrong, Stephanie Covington. (2009). *Not All Black Girls Know How to Eat: A Story of Bulimia*.
Bacon, J. (2011). Culturally responsive poetry. *Journal of Poetry Therapy* 24, 1-15.
Brown, D. and Keith, V. (2003). *In and out of our right minds: The mental health of African American women*. New York: Columbia University Press.
Cooper, A. (1892). *A voice from the South, By a Black woman of the South*. Docs South. Retrieved 2 January, 2015 from http://docsouth.unc.edu/church/cooper/cooper.html.
Evans, S. Y., Bell Thomas, K. and Burton, N. Eds. (forthcoming). *Black Women's Mental Health:*

---

[15] Systematic Sexual Violence by U. S. State Agencies: A Victimology Approach. PhD Dissertation. Sarah Brightman, Western Michigan University, 2011.
[16] Dedication of Peace Benches at Clark Atlanta University, http://theburtonwire.com/2015/03/27/news/iconic-poet-sonia-sanchez-honored-with-peace-benches/.
Purple Pens Poetry Workshops for Survivors of Sexual Violence http://www.purplepens.net/. Accessed July 10, 2015.

Balancing Strength and Vulnerability. Under review.

Evans, S. Y. (2015) "Healing Traditions in Black Women's Writing: Resources for Poetry Therapy." *Journal of Poetry Therapy*. vol. 28, no. 3 July, pp. 1-14.

Evans, S. Y. (2014). "Inner lions: Definitions of peace in Black women's memoirs: A Strength-based model for mental health." *Peace Studies Journal, 7*(2), 1-30.

Evans, S. Y. (2013). Sesheta.net. Database of 500 Africana Women's Memoirs. http://www.sesheta.net/

International Federation for Biblio/Poetry Therapy. (2012). *Guide to training requirements for certification and registration in poetry therapy*.

Lenhart, J. (2006). Trying to break a 'culture of silence' on rape. *Washington Post*. Retrieved 2 January, 2015 from http://www.washingtonpost.com/wp-dyn/content/article/2006/05/29/AR2006052901012.html

Lorde, A. (1984). Poetry is not a luxury. *Sister Outsider*. (pp. 37-39). Freedom, CA: Crossing Press.

Mazza, N. (2012). Poetry/creative writing for an arts and athletics community outreach program for at-risk youth. *Journal of Poetry Therapy* 25, 225-231.

-----. (2013). *Poetry Therapy: Theory and Practice: Theory and Practice*. Taylor and Francis.

Sirleaf, E. J. (2009). *This child will be great: Memoir of a remarkable life by Africa's first woman president*. New York: Harper Collins.

Co-Editor Introduction

Voices: The Audacity

Sharnell Myles, Psy. D.
Care Clinician, youthSpark

They had the audacity to believe that no one would tell. That s*he*, inside of her childlike body, would stay isolated, afraid, unspoken, and fragmented. They had the audacity to threaten, to beat, to enter her without permission, to exploit, to control while falsely believing that they had won. They were wrong! Nicole was a beautiful 18-year old who recounted her story of multiple sexual assaults and trafficking as she held tears in her eyes:

> …Why did they take me? Why did they have to kidnap me, beat me, have sex with me like that? All I could do was close my eyes. My body was there but I forced my mind into to a safe place. My body still experiences those days but I don't understand those feelings.[17]

I did not have the answers. Nicole was sexually assaulted by her mother's friend from 7 to 12-years of age. At 13 she was kidnapped and exploited by many men who saw her as an object, not the 13-year old who wanted to be outside with her friends jumping rope or skating. At 14-years of age, she was sexually assaulted by someone who she thought she knew. She was traumatized and no one understood. Nicole's experience has become all too familiar for me as a trauma specialist. *Purple Sparks* is a breakthrough, a Voice, the beginning of a journey for many sexual assault survivors. Just like many poets in this book, Nicole decided to be unafraid and take the first step toward a journey of healing. History has taught us that atrocities cannot be buried, just as the echoes of a voice cannot be silenced.

Voices

Purple Sparks is a chorus of voices that refused to be silenced. The 1970's women's liberation movement brought about awareness to violence against women and continues to bring consciousness to the effects of sexual assault. We as a people have learned that secrets are no longer okay and that the only way to begin the journey of healing is to speak about, what was once thought to be the most unspeakable stories to ever tell, sexual assault. This book contains some of the most powerful voices (poems) by sexual assault survivors – women, men, and young girls alike. The poets have granted readers the *privilege* to hear their voices, to walk alongside them on their journeys of pain, betrayal, dissociation, power, and love as they restore healing and bring meaning to their experiences.

The voices of children echo throughout this anthology and are represented with poems such as *Yummy Pearl, Free Style, and Untitled Living*. These poems were created by young girls who know firsthand the destructive nature of sexual assault. Yummy Pearl lays out the realities of a 17-year old girl who once compared herself to a slave. She believed her soul was controlled by someone she thought to be a god - her pimp. Free Style was written by a 15-year old girl who dared herself to say yes to life, to admonish her beauty, and to understand that the price for her life was already paid by Christ even after three sexual assaults. Collectively, these young girls, 13 to 17-years of age, have found their voices even in the midst of intergenerational trauma, exploitation, poverty, and abuse. In Untitled Living, life has taken on a new meaning of hope, love, strength, beauty, and freedom. The courage to revisit fragments of their sexual assault gave power to their ability to

---

[17] Interview with Nicole, September 25, 2015. Quote used with permission of Nicole.

preserve a sense of trust and control in a world that was once unpredictable and traumatizing. Their motto: Yesterday I found my voice, Today I'm here to shout about it!

The power of love
In today's time, we have to ask ourselves, "What manner of chaos is this in the lives of our children?" as it relates to sexual assault. From sexual abuse to child sex trafficking, perpetrators are working overtime to silence the next generation through modern day slavery.

As a child my parents cared for many children who were in the Philadelphia foster care system and adopted four. This was my introduction to love triumphing trauma. Children who were savagely beaten, sexually assaulted by strangers and parents and wounded to their cores were being introduced to unconditional love while living in our home. We, the family, had to learn through the trauma and make a conscious effort to understand that abuse did not mean the end. I believe that this new home for them exuded forgiveness and unconditional positive regard which precipitated a degree of conscious forgiveness resulting in the ultimate sacrifice– forgiving those who hurt them. They were given the chance to learn about real love - Love that heals, love that forgives, love that permeates so deep into the soul that reconciliation began and hardened hearts dissolved.

For over sixteen years I have had women tell me that pairing love and trauma in the same sentence was an oxymoron. It has been said that there remains a void in the crux of love and trust even after the therapeutic work has begun. However, we all have the innate ability to heal and love, just as we have the innate ability to bring forth language in many forms. We hold the resources, the boundaries, the permission to restore power and the capacity to understand how to use that power in our own healing. That same power overflows as we find and use our voices, individually and collectively.

Together we *will* bring forth a resounding boldness in the fight to bring awareness to sexual assault and to end child sex trafficking. That is the power of love!

Purple Sparks
Poetry by Survivors of Sexual Violence

Contributors

1. Tina A — 24
2. Cole B — 25
3. Thomaesa B — 26
4. Emily B — 28
5. Bethany B — 29
6. Michele B — 32
7. Bittersweet — 35
8. Stephanie B — 37
9. Donna C — 38
10. Denise C — 39
11. Deborah C — 40
12. Amber C — 41
13. Brian C — 43
14. Cailey C — 45
15. Christine Marie — 47
16. Daniel de C — 49
17. Julie C — 51
18. Tiffani D — 52
19. Arika E — 53
20. Miranda E — 55
21. Jacqueline F — 57
22. Amber F — 58
23. Tafui F — 60
24. Leslee Ann F — 62
25. Jane G — 65
26. Erika G — 66
27. Arden H — 68
28. Robin H — 70
29. Angela K — 71
30. Chong K — 73
31. Toby K — 77
32. Diane L — 79
33. Diamante L — 82
34. Jannina L — 84
35. Marie Louise — 88
36. Sherese M — 89
37. Kio M — 91
38. Valerie M — 92
39. Debra M — 94
40. Polly M — 95
41. Patricia — 96
42. April R — 99
43. Maria S — 101
44. Ashley S — 105
45. Adriana S — 106
46. Marilyn T — 107
47. Sylvia T — 108
48. Wil T — 109
49. Diva T — 110
50. Mercedes W — 113
51. Rachael W — 115
52. Tania W — 117
53. youthSpark Voices — 118

Tina A
Tina A lives in Michigan. She is a 39 year survivor of childhood molestation at the hands of a neighbor and his two accomplices. Married for 23 years, a mother of two and a business owner, she spends her free time reading, caring for her family and two dogs. She enjoys boxing, running and travel.

A Survivors Haiku
Fighting for myself
Against fear, shame, doubt, memories
Victorious me

A Different Me
Often, I have worried
How would the experience be
If I were a different me
One with a childhood unhurried
Where my heart is light, without fury
Easy, breezy, carefree
Memories crisp, clear, not blurry
Mostly, all was not meant to be
The criminal touch of his hand
Innocence, never was mine
From five to forty-four
Anger, constricts like steel bands
By victim, I am not be defined
My name is survivor, forevermore

Cole B
I am a survivor of childhood abuse, sexual abuse and domestic violence, due to the trauma as a child resulted in P.T.S.D- (Post Traumatic Stress Disorder). I also have D.I.D (Dissociation Identity Disorder) formally know as M.P.D. (Multiple Personality Disorder) or as I like to say D.I.G (Dissociative Identity Gift) I am breaking my silence and sharing some poetry with you.

Rock
I rock myself
As the pain
Consumes me
As the ache
breathes though me
The tears that fall
As I cry out for all
To hear me.
Lips that shiver
A heart that quavers
Tingling mingling
All in me
When will it stop
As I hide from
The shame
That devours me
When will I live
To endure what was taken
As I fall
To the floor
Sobbing
In my pain
As fire within
Burns me
Consumes me
In the end
I rock myself

I won
You took my innocence,
you stole my childhood,
you tried to break me
by taking me,
you hurt my body,
you tore my heart,
you tried to take my soul
your rage took over
I tried to run
the more I fought
the more you won
then I discovered
     my mind had a world

a place
deep inside
I could hide
A beautiful place
where no one could go
a place that was safe
and I could call my own
you tried to break
all of me
You thought
you won
in the end
you failed
miserably
for my mind
rescued me
In the end
I won

Forgiveness
Jesus my savior
One day I will ride
to the sky
I am eager,
To be in your arms
No more hurts,
no more pain.
No more hiding.
Forgiveness you gave
Now I must do the same.
My chains are strong
My anger holds on
Take this darkness
From my heart
Take this pain
Let me let go
Let kindness begin.
From God above,
Asking you
to remain true
I can only pray
justice will prevail
And God's mighty
Sword will swing upon the evil
That bestowed me as a child
Until then I must seek
To forgive,
Pray for their soul.
Forgiveness
Jesus my Savior.

Thomaesa B

<u>Untitled</u>
Yesterday, I rose.
Today, I am learning to think.
Tomorrow, I'll move.

<u>The Movement</u>
It starts with silence.
It swells up to a mumble.
It ends with a shout.

Emily B
Emily B is completing her PhD in English literature at a university, and she writes poetry and short prose in Ontario, Canada. Emily has a special passion for social justice and the way in which it can be read and translated artistically through poetry and other forms of art and literature. She believes that encouraging and enabling oppressed voices to be heard is the first step in enacting pragmatic and judicial change in the world. In her spare time, Emily enjoys hiking, long drives down country back roads, and singing when no one's home. Her poetry has recently appeared in *Blueprint Magazine* and *Guide to Kulchur Creative Journal*.

Talking Cure
I had a tattoo scratched down my arm
black flames scorched my outer angle
Each set of eyes that passed would grimace and confirm
        "yes, you must have this removed"
The idea of being clean again
The child's face fell upwards into mine
cheeks gushing clear glass
plastered permanently wet:
        "I had a nightmare about you"
We can't find an adult to help us
and frustrated tears stretch to waking
accompanying a spinning grasping freeze
Use your grounding technique:
I am steam pouring over the edge of the bath tub
I am boiling to the surface a floating dumpling
ready to be lifted out and buttered
nothing, everywhere
wrecked

Descend
I am the gap in your arching, soft neck
your warm, pooling skin
My hands are here
my fingers dig through your skin, past your sinews and bones
and I reach through to my thighs
My thighs are here
                          not here
then my brain is an anvil that crushes my blood
and I shrivel retreat   run
I swaddle myself in folding blankets
a fetus born on a faux-velvet red recliner
How can this image sit next to a sunset, incompatible?
How can I feel that your hands are love again?
I don't say this to bother you, to ask you for an answer
I don't say this to show you
I say this because I have to say
and say
despite the boiling vomit rising
and the aching faux-velvet red creeping to fill my edges
and the nightmares and the freeze
I write this because I told myself this
was the only thing I could not write.

Bethany B
Bethany B was born and raised in Westmoreland, Jamaica. She earned a teacher's diploma and is a First Class Honours graduate of a university in the West Indies. She is currently an established educator and actress. To date, she has been featured in approximately 10 stage productions playing for audiences in Jamaica and the Caribbean, Canada, England, and The United States. She has also done a number of screen work including two sitcoms and two television drama series, one of which was the popular "The Blackburns of Royal Palm". She has also done a number of television and radio commercials in addition to appearing in a radio serial drama. Natalee 'co-wrote' the adaptation of James Baldwin's play "Amen Corner" and wrote several of the original songs that were used in the said production. She has penned numerous short stories and poems that feature themes that cater to young adult audiences such as friendship, loss, and love & romance. Natalee enjoys theatrical entertainment, board games, athletic meets, and exercising. Currently, she teaches at a college in Kingston and lectures at a university in West Indies while she completes her PhD in Linguistics.

<u>Crazed Memories</u>
I will never forget how you ravaged me...
stole my soul and left my body an empty bleeding tomb.
I shall always remember the death your eyes spoke to me
As you drained my mortality.
The memories of the ruin you evoked in my cavern tumble restlessly in my head.
I will never get away from the whispers that chase me, bar me in... threaten my sanity.
Escape... how can I?
Disappear... I want to!!
Die... I have!!!
A thousand times too many I have crawled and climbed into myself
But I see the same scene... the same----
It never changes!
You say it doesn't matter...
It shouldn't...
Right!!!
You don't understand the path I walk
Seeing myself... wishing I didn't.
Seeing myself seeing you... wishing I couldn't!
I shall never forget as I will always remember
I wish I could die
but I can't
I am already dead!!

<u>Dear Mr. Rapist</u>
I watched you climb into me, felt my silent tears scorch my cheeks as it splattered its way onto your terrorist arms.
My body struggled in reprisal, but was defeated by your man's strength.
My shamed soul closed its eyes in sleep unwilling to be witness to you murdering my innocence.
I died a thousand deaths that night as you savagely spilled your unwelcomed seed, unsterilizing my womb.
You shattered my world with your debauchery.
In abjection, I watched you 'reclothe' yourself and walk away with my existence.
Limp and listless I lay cold and empty
I did not wish to know me.

Mentally, I began divorcing me from myself.
Finally when I dared to move, I was faced with the mirror on the wall staring at me with accusing eyes.
I confronted that stranger and saw... you... your spirit, curdling inside me; and I lashed out!
My pain ripping and tearing and smashing those demon eyes that threatened to imprison me.
Spent, I stood soullessly watching the shards of glass splinter in parallel to the destruction you wrought in my life.
I have waited to confront you. I've waited to kill you. I hate you.
I hate me.
I hate myself hating you.
I hate the me you created when you killed the me I loved
I hate that I hate.
I wish I could forgive…
forgive you, forgive myself.
But I cannot forgive because I cannot forget.
Your stench is forever implanted in me, and so I live with you, a bitter memory hanging around my neck like a cursed talisman.

Sometimes I Cry
Sometimes I cry
not because I hurt but because I can't forget
I can't forget the fear, the panic that set in when I saw the intent in his eyes;
The chuckle he made when I thought I was about to die
Sometimes, I cry
Sometimes I cry
Not because I am sad but because I can't be happy
The scar left by his sadistic actions is a constant memory that keeps paranoia at my door;
I try to heal, to let go, move on but each hurdle crossed presents one more
Sometimes, I cry
Sometimes I cry
Not because of pain but because of a deep-seated sorrow;
I hear his voice still; like a taunting mantra it reverberates in my head,
The scent of his flesh in my nostrils fuels my dread
Sometimes, I cry
Sometimes I cry
Not because I am hurt but because I am burdened
Burdened with shame, with guilt, with memories whose link I cannot sever
I recall his lips smiling in satisfaction at my pleas which seemed to fuel his pleasure
Sometimes I cry
Not because I am weak but because I have to be strong
Strong enough to not let the memories consume and destroy me
To not let hate for one man destroy my faith in all humanity
Strong enough not to lash out when that is all I want to do
Strong enough to know that my tears are therapeutic too
Sometimes
I cry.
I cry.
I cry.
I am crying.

Revengicide

Daily I travel through this tunnel of darkness
chased by a beating heart pounding to escape its cage
I'm caged... caged and crazy
Light is my kryptonite I must escape its *illuminescence*
must not allow my truths to be revealed as lies tidied up in my existence to hide my fears.
I'm consciously inducing comatose
so my subconscious can take over
making me unresponsible for my Achilles' heel
that will allow me to succumb to the darkness that beckons
for me to avenge what must be.
My burdensome heart will not rest in my bosom but beats brutally against this barricade that has it caged
Caged... caged and crazy.
Crazy is my mind that never sleeps but stalks the dark sinister streets
Hoping to find peace
Peace of mind...
Peace and tranquillity
Piece of the missing puzzle
... piece...
To use....
I'm a vigilante
Led by this craziness that has heated the blood coursing through my wicked wilful heart.
The darkness suffocates my soul yet comforts me... strange
my chi has been disturbed
I'm a mere ghoul empty and emotionless
I am fickle and faithless
Loyal only to my aim
And I will aim...

Michele B
Michele B was operations manager for an international fitness chain before leaving her 20-year career in the fitness industry to follow her heart and write: about women and trauma, about the mixed-race experience, and about the art of finding oneself. In 2012, she co-produced a student-run event entitled Shades of Silence in Trauma: Women of Color Reclaiming our Voices in collaboration with a Pan African Studies Department at a university in California, which included personal testimonies of women of color, a panel, and resources to promote healing and self-empowerment for women experiencing and/or recovering from trauma. She was featured in a short documentary on rape and trauma. Currently, she is researching her family's mixed-race history and writing their fascinating story. She is associate editor for *Kapu-Sens: The Literary Journal of the Africana Studies* and her work has been published in *Bloom, poeticdiversity, Metamorphoses, Triathlete*, and in a forthcoming anthology on women in the Black Power Movement. She lives in Southern California with her life partner.

HEAT
On the blackest desert nights when I believe
for certain that no one loves me, I despise
my piano, with its ebony and ivory
keys, and the beautiful melodies

that burst from the voluptuous violet-blues
of the hydrangeas on my vanity; I cannot bear
the sight of perfectly-curled corkscrews,
and I especially hate successful black women—

especially my mother.
When I am certain I am unloved, I like
nothing better than to burn things,
especially the telephone lines, my teeth,
and your flesh. What's the matter with you?

they always ask indignantly,
as I grind my fingers to the bone.
On these hot nights, I like to sit naked
in the vastness of my parched, private desert,

and revel in the heat of my burns,
spread-eagle, under a cloudlessly hot indigo sky.
These are the razorsharp moments when I know
that I won the foxhunt: you, my love, cannot kill me—
I already have.

LITTLE MIXED MARY AND THE TIGER IN THE JUNGLE

Once upon a time, there was a little girl who was barely fifteen, and her name was Mary.
She had curly brown hair and big brown eyes, and barely-brown skin.
And her black mother divorced her white dad, and then her mother got a black boyfriend.
But Mary's mother was very busy, because she had four kids to raise while working full-time,
    so she never had time to sew Mary any clothes.

And Mary liked to buy her own clothes at the Northridge Mall anyway; she never bought a beautiful red coat, but she did buy a pair of beautiful blue trousers.
And since they'd moved to arid southern California, she didn't need a beautiful umbrella, green or otherwise.
But she loved shoes, so she bought a beautiful pair of purple high-heels, with crimson soles and crimson linings.
And then wasn't Little Mixed Mary just grand (not), all mixedup and lost and vulnerable,
Because her parents were too gone themselves to be there for her.

So Mary put on her brave new face and her fine new clothes and took her brown self out, into the thick white Jungle of the San Fernando Valley.
And by and by, she met her mother's new boyfriend, because he moved in.
He thought he was a Tiger, but he really was a Sewer Rat.
He thought he looked grand, in a yellow-striped tiger's coat, but really he looked like a villainous perp.
And her mother cooked him a delicious breakfast of pancakes and bacon, even though she was too busy to cook for her own kids.
And the Tiger went into Mary's room late one night, where she was safely tucked in and sleeping in her pink-hearted jammies, and he said to her,
"Your mother and I discussed it, and we both agreed that this would be best for you."
And Little Mixed Mary was so scared, she didn't know what to say or do at all, so she just did nothing.

And the Tiger said, "Very well," and then he raped her, with relish.
Then the Tiger got through with poor Little Mixed Mary, and he went away saying,
"Now, I'm the most grand *and* the most cunning Tiger in the Jungle!"

And poor Little Mixed Mary stayed there crying, because she didn't know how to find her way out of her parched, private desert, while her mother pretended nothing happened.
Because her mother didn't know what to do with Mary, she didn't know what to do at all.

Presently, Mary learned that the Tiger was back in the crappy parts of L.A., no doubt into other evil things. She heard through the jungle that the Tiger had gotten caught cheating with another man's wife, and he had gotten what he deserved by the other man.
She imagined with relish that the Tiger had wrangled and scrambled and found himself running round and round a tree.
And he ran faster and faster, so fast that you couldn't see his legs at all,
so fast that he just melted away, and there was nothing left but a big pool of melted ghee.

And the other man saw all the melted ghee, and he said, "Oh! What lovely melted ghee! I'll send it to Little Mixed Mary, for her mother to cook with."
When Little Mixed Mary's mother saw the melted ghee, she was so pleased!
"Now," she said, "we'll all have pancakes for breakfast!"
She put on her white apron, the one with the yellow-striped Hello Kittys on it, and she made a huge plate of lovely pancakes, and she smothered them with melted ghee.

And Little Mixed Mary sat down to breakfast with her mother and her brothers and sister.
And her mother ate twenty-seven pancakes,
And her brothers and sister each ate fifty-five, but Little Mixed Mary ate a hundred and sixty-nine,
Because she was so very hungry.

YOU SEEMED LIKE SUCH A FRIENDLY BACKHOE
Dear C,

You were so handsome
with your shiny chrome fenders and your black monster tires.
I thought we might get hitched.

But then you belched
black diesel smoke, and your monster
tires assaulted my bones

crushing them one by one.
First you mangled my femur, then
driving in reverse, apologized.

Initially I forgave you, which
is precisely when you shifted into overdrive
and crushed my pelvis. You raised your metal jaws menacingly

your engine whining in a high-pitched laugh
until it shuddered and stalled with a sob.
I couldn't leave fast enough

so you made one final pass
with your pistons knocking
razing my spine and scoring

my quivering heart
with the tread of your monster tires.

Bittersweet
Inspired by my paternal grandmother and great aunt, I identify as a Black womanist with Afrocentric feminist tendencies. As a transpersonal psychologist advancing toward my doctorate, I place myself in the in-between spaces of mind, body, spirit, and culture. My work primarily focuses on the cosmology and wholeness of Africana womanhood with a profound emphasis on sacred stories. Capturing, contemplating and conjuring the soul qualities embedded in the lived and voiced experience is my divine rite, exposing these gifts to the academy is my scholarly endeavor. I lecture on diversity, Black psychology, and culturally appropriate therapeutic skills. Additionally, I have presented the lived experiences of Alice Coltrane and Sojourner Truth, as well as the essence of womanist psychological wisdom. Utilizing a multimedia platform I address the needs of my audience to captivate and impress the value of African-centeredness as a primary influence. I am a doctoral fellow for the *International Journal of Transpersonal Studies* and I have two scholarly contributions in press. I served two years on the Association of Black Psychologists Student Circle Board of Directors as their inaugural western region graduate student representative. As a board member I hosted what is considered the first Afrocentric Transpersonal conference in 2012. When time permits I invest extracurricular hours to appreciating spoken word, musical concerts, and motherhood. Poetry is a lifeline.

Dance
Navy blue stripped one piece
Running through sprinklers
Hankering for one more candy necklace
Glorifying the sun in a bucket of ice tea

Claiming cars driving down a two-way road
Humming the blues off a 45
Oh those days of innocence weren't long
Snatched by a distant in-law
Godless, lonely and beer bellied

My panties' blossoms browned
Sliding to another side of the shared bed
Silently guilty and tainted
Longing for home, safety

Voicelessness was a safety net
Broken silence replaced by shame 'cause I was a *liar*
Violated by the disbelief
Home dismantled by a tattered and torturous love

Cried for affection
Ran toward neighborhood brethren
Corrupted by naïveté and juvenile substitutes
Traded sprinklers for back alleys

Soiled soul, screamless dreams and frigid excommunication
No mirrors, no selfies
Not good enough for anything but anger
Preservation was antithetical

Overprotective weight wraps my mistrust
Familial direction too little, way too late

Praises to the All Mighty and forgiveness are saviors
Prayer, poetry, vocal prose punctuate redemption

My motherhood blessed a do-over
Pass on the learnings
Unconditional love begins to spread the inner innocent's agenda
Memories of kites, hopscotch, and rain dancing
Finally reign supreme

Stephanie B
I am a 43 year-old wife, mother, teacher and student. Thirteen years ago I was raped by two martial arts instructors I was supposed to be able to trust. Because I was drugged the evidence was gone before I could press charges, though I did file a police report. Just a year after the rape my family and I moved to another state. Through faith, family support, writing and counseling I have found healing and forgiveness. In the time since the attack I have graduated from college and found my calling teaching middle school social studies.

<u>Changes</u>
The winds of change are hurricanes spinning through my life,
Barreling like a freight train toward a final destination.
Everything in their path is sucked into the vortex of the storm,
Leaving behind only the splintered pieces of what used to be.
As merciless as a summer storm that cannot be contained,
These winds of change.

Donna C, Good Eagle Woman
I was SXA violated at a Native medical center in Alaska and when I reported it, instead of justice and punishment to the sexual predator, the police department took me to an emergency room where I was beaten. I was held against my will, my civil rights were violated and there is now a federal case pending.

I am an Alaska native artist, a mother, and grandmother, honest, law abiding person with extremely high morals and credentials. I was held for eight days in 2013 and my civil rights were violated by the three day clause in the law and finally I went before a judge. I won the case and my freedom was given back to me. But I was SXA at a hospital and they tried very hard to cover it up, and I have gotten absolutely NO JUSTICE to date. The scales of justice do not balance for Alaska women, especially Alaska Natives, that we can't deny, always get the worst treatment in the judicial system.

PREDATOR
you violated my Vagina
you tried to put it all behind ya
by telling lies to all your colleagues
tried to dis me like a folly

You put a zapper in your hand dude
and pressed it hard with a demon attitude
you had your nurse say "she felt that"
to make you feel like a cool cat.

What you are is a PREDATOR
But you think you're the guy next door
Hope the judge pounds you to the floor
My tribe waits with a single lude
A broken Squaw can be very rude

I walk in cold with Tribal justice
I went to cops to cry injustice
Instead they took me back to DIE
Beat down and left bleeding at ---

They tried to say that I was crazy
disillusioned, ill and kind of lazy
They never met me but still they see
a low life spicehead Indian lady

Predators have no place in society
They break us down with anxiety
To make life safe for our children
molesters freedom has to come to the end.

Because the brave Squaw came forward
She will face and debase that coward
Now he'll be living in the system
So he can't make another Victim.

Thank God.

Denise C

<u>The Pattern</u>
Curled beneath the coverlet
cocooned in quilted down
I fight the heavy tug of sleep
with all my edges honed.

Watery moonlight thins the darkness
pooled in every corner.
Shadows puddle on the ceiling
drawn with clumsy charcoal fingers.

My fears congeal like curdled milk
as footfalls whisper
from the hallway
hissing his arrival.

Smothered by the smell of smoke
and cloying breath of rum
I fold myself into the space
between the bed and wall.

Bedclothes rustle, slide like snakes
the sheets are pulled aside.
Taking flight while holding still
I disconnect myself.

Witness from a distance,
unmoved by his touch:
the sweaty hands and scratchy beard
and lips and tongue and teeth.

I count rosebuds in the curtains
until this weight has lifted.

<u>The Limits of Misery</u>
You long for a past you didn't have / the way your tongue keeps finding
empty space that once held a tooth / surprised to find it gone and certain it will return.

<u>Retreat</u>
I am filled with noisy
jangled scraps,
the roar and tumult
of broken childhood..

I must vacuum out
this knotted clatter,
old ricochets
of damaged days.

And once I am empty / I will arm myself / with silence.

Deborah C

Deborah C., is an Assistant Professor of Sociology at a university in South Carolina. Her interests include: gender-based violence, the body, creative nonfiction, and feminist pedagogy. As a scholar-teacher-activist, Dr. C has done domestic violence work in three states with survivors and perpetrators. She serves on the Board of Directors of a coalition against domestic violence and sexual assault in South Carolina. In addition, she serves as an expert consultant in legal cases involving sexual violence. She is working on book-length projects regarding what it means to teach about intimacy and violence, and about providing care for ill and elderly parents.

A Rage Against/ From the Female Body
Really fucked up
This thing called violence against women
Strange that women are violated every day, raped and strangled
Dismembered, thrown in trunks and dumpsters
Tied with rope to the side windows of cars, fucked in the ass with pipes and tire irons
And when the women fight back with rage the weight of a sledgehammer
The context of the violence against them is rendered invisible and their rage is all that is visible
Why is it that yesterday in the nail salon I called a woman tiny
To speak of her in-shape body and she remarked that
That was the second time she was called tiny in the same day
And then I watched as the woman got pleasure
From people thinking of her as tiny
Because we women are supposed to be small, take up less space
And the woman tied with rope to the car window and fucked in the ass
Was really too large for the man she was trying to resist.

Amber C
My name is Amber Lynn C and I am a survivor of child abuse, sexual assault, and homelessness. I was born and raised in Minnesota and I am now 22 years old. My life experiences have shaped who I am as a person and I am driven to fight back against the injustice that myself and many others have experienced. Despite all the odds I never gave up as a kid when I was being abused. I had a strong will to work hard, I was convinced if I was good enough at a number of things then I'd eventually get taken out of my situation. When I was 17 years, old my stepfather attempted to have sex with me. I fought back and his attempt was unsuccessful. I reported him to the county's battered women resources center and an investigation was conducted. At the end of it the social worker assigned to my case told me there was no motive. So I never had a case. My family told me I misunderstood my stepfather's intentions. As a result I am obtaining a four year degree in humans services, a minor in psychology, and become a police officer to help my community in any way that I can.

<u>I am Gone</u>
I was 17 when it happened.
I had become nervous, wary, and sickened when I was left in a room with you.
I didn't know why, but I do now.
You observed and stalked me for two years, and now you were ready to snap your trap.
You came in one night like a dark silent shadow of prey, hunting me.
The look in your eyes was one of hunger and excitement.
My skin prickled and my insides became chilled.
This can't be happening I thought.
Your hands reached for me and you trapped me in your arms.
You squeezed my arms tight to my body and my mind screamed.
I struggled to break your hold and like an anaconda you constricted even tighter.
It was hard to breathe, my arms rendered useless.
My throat was filled with a foul taste and I couldn't utter a sound.
You leaned in with a predatory smile to claim my lips.
You wanted to mark me as yours.
I jerked my face away as far as I could.
Your lips met the flesh of my neck and it seared skin.
My stomach roiled, my skin burned, and my blood turned to ice.
The fear bound spell on me shattered to a thousand pieces.
New found strength spread through me like a tornado and a yell of rage and disgust tore from my throat.
My head swung like a deadly blade and I drew blood from you.
You snarled the rage of a twisted monster and lunged.
My hand became a fist of stone, your nose crunched like an egg and warm, sticky, red blood dripped down your face.
A voice like thunder boomed out orders.
Don't ever touch me again! Don't ever come near me again! You sick bastard!
That voice commanded obedience and it was more lethal than an ice storm.
The man I once thought of as Daddy lost it's human form.
His face no longer showed kindness, in its place was mindless hunger for power, control, and an appetite for the forbidden.
This oily, grotesque, dark form slunk away from my bed. Hate burned in its eyes.
It hissed venomously at me and slipped out the door.
My heart hammered like a scared rabbit narrowly avoiding death.
The contents of my stomach came up and burned my throat.
My body shivered like a leaf blowing through fierce winds and I barred my door with everything I could find.

I would not allow that creature, that thing, to come after me a second time.
Then I broke from the inside out. Uncontrollable sobs ripped from my body and I cursed at myself.
I froze! Why had my voice choked?! The unimaginable almost happened.
But it didn't happen. I'm still whole. My body is still mine. I'm still alive.
I will fight this. I promised myself. *I will make him pay. I will take him down.*
But I never did. I was told there was no motive. It was just a "misunderstanding".
I feel sick. I feel alone. My voice is gone. I am gone.

<u>What is It Like to be Sexually Assaulted?</u>
What is it like for the victim after they have been sexually assaulted?
They feel sick inside because someone kissed them and ran greedy hands down their body.
They feel powerless and ashamed because someone forced arousal from their bodies without their consent.
They scan their surroundings all the time now, making sure that no one is following them.
They jump when they hear loud noises.
And if someone touches them from behind their fight or flight kicks into overdrive.
They don't trust as easily anymore.
They expect the worst from people that show an interest in them.
They worry they'll be assaulted again.
They cry late at night because they don't want to be afraid anymore.
They feel isolated from everyone else, they're wary and less carefree as their peers.
What is it like for the victim after they've been assaulted?
They're lonely, terrified, sad, hurt, confused, and lost.
They want to be loved but they're afraid they'll re-live their assault again.
They wish being hugged didn't make them feel uneasy, especially if it's people they're close to.
They have nightmares, flashbacks, and it all feels so real.
Hands painfully grip your arms, hot breath hits your face, you're pinned to the wall and you can't get away.
Your clothes are being pulled off and you're not strong enough to stop what's happening.
Why do I know these things?
Because I was sexually assaulted.
And I reported it.
Nothing was done.
My voice went unheard.
My struggle meant nothing to the court.
I was told I misunderstood my attacker's intentions.
His arms pinning mine down and trying to kiss me when I said no is not confusing.
The force he used to subdue me was not imagined.
What is it like to be a victim of sexual assault?
It's degrading, terrifying, and sickening.
Our communities should be helping victims, not shaming them.
They should listen instead of ignoring them.
We're your classmates, your friends, and your loved ones.
You shouldn't look away.
Please help.
I want to be a survivor, not a victim.
So please, learn compassion, learn empathy.
Our world can become a better place if we just help each other.
So let's help each other.

Brian C

Brian C is a Bigfoot that exists in the real world, but, like Bigfoot, no one's gotten a clear photo of him yet. He is a survivor of sexual assault and a child abuse survivor. Brian was six years old when he lived through his first sexual assault. His father left the family that same year. Living on his own by the time he was 15, Brian nearly froze to death in the street on his first night homeless. But Brian knew that if he managed to survive that night he could find the strength to continue surviving one day at a time. Today, Brian is an artist, an accomplished chef and an inspirational speaker.

Brian passionately encourages and facilitates open conversations in groups of men and women who have also survived abuse as a child or young adult. He begins these conversations by speaking about his own traumatic experiences and outlining his journey from victim to survivor to artist to inspirational speaker. Brian was formerly a professional chef and hotel executive. He seeks innovative ways to raise money and rally communities in support of the fight against childhood sexual assault. Brian also leverages his art as a resource in helping each child. He is an OVC consultant and Rape Abuse, Incest National Network (RAINN) speaker. He has been featured in Ripple Effects of Child Sexual Assault; a documentary about abuse survival. Brian is currently working on getting his first book, *Struggling to Fight*, published.

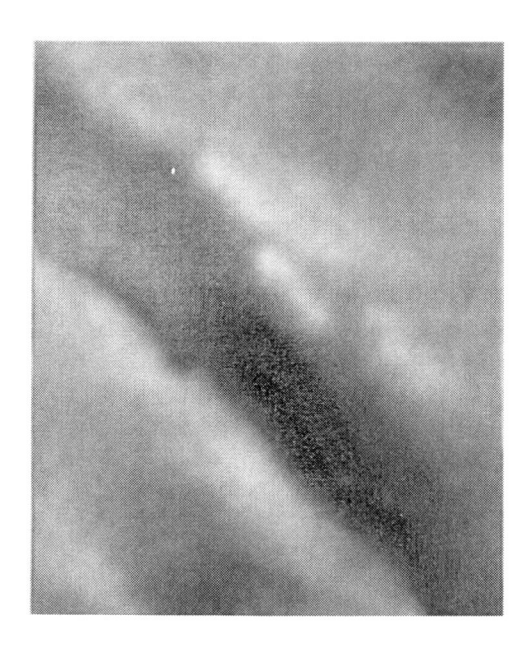

<u>Who I was is still who I am</u>

I was visible once, I was seen
I was innocent once. I was a child
I was visible till someone saw me, and stole my childhood
I was destroyed, I was molded
I was a toy, I was a recreated
I was destroyed by someone, who turned me into a toy
I was afraid, I was brave
I was doubtful, I was confident
I was confident that I was afraid
I was in a building, I was broken
I was afraid, I would be seen

I was afraid because I was broken
I became visible and I was a child
I am recreated, I was no longer his toy
I am doubtful, I will be confident
But I will be BRAVE because I WAS BROKEN

<u>Why I am proud I am a survivor of sexual assault</u>
Why is it weird to hear or read those words, is it the connection to such a personal attack that makes you turn your head in shame of our discourse to hear.
Is it the fact that people wonder if they could handle such an event, I can tell you I never asked this because I never knew different.
Let me tell you why people should not be afraid to discuss survival, without the deeds done to me I would not be who I am NOW and who I am is part of that.
Why am I proud of being a sexual, physical, and mental abuse survivor, suffering those deeds to me have made me stubborn
Being stubborn is truly one of the greatest feeling, knowing you cannot beat me, knowing you can do no more to me then what I have already endured.
Imagine living a life where you already know that nothing worse can be done to you, imagine the freedom of that thought.
Being stubborn has saved my life, on December 14. 1989 when I was sleeping in a car in Anchorage Alaska I knew if I could survive that night and not freeze then the worst was almost over.
The lesson I have learned from being a survivor, dedication I am more single minded on goals than most people why because I learned how to concentrate and focus.
I had to concentrate to forget what happened and I had to focus to know that I would only move forward if I forgave.
I have learned many thing in this life the value of a friend and how to trust a person not because you're born of them but because you have chosen to trust in them.
All these lessons would never have existed to the level they do if I had not been assaulted. So ask me if I would change these deeds done to me and I will shout out to the world" NO and bring it."
So when someone states they are a survivor don't look on them with total pity, just know that one day they will discover the freedom of being stubborn, dedicated, and given trust.
If you know people who need to see this please share and like but most importantly share someone somewhere is wondering if anything good can come from this.

Cailey C
Cailey C was born in Texas. She grew up playing soccer, spending time with friends and family, saving the environment, and laughing. She is currently a 22 year old student at a university in California, majoring in Biology. She also enjoys dancing, singing, piano, traveling, and writing.

White Flower
If there was a choice,
I would return back to that night,
to relinquish a resounding fight.
The sun is disappearing,
it is dusk.
I can hear the storm coming,
I can smell his skin of musk.
In one of my hands I hold a white flag,
in the other I grip a fist,
I try to free myself from his grip,
but now it is too late to resist.

My white dress was ripped off in the depth of the night,
can you hear my silent screams and my desolate fight?
His sadistic eyes forced me to stare,
and wallow in my own despair.
Was his intention pure or for power?
Or was I just a victim of the hour.

I was a lovely daughter of the man who caused me pain,
                              now this flower has wilted and ruined in the rain.

Ceremonial
Oh rock-a-by ba-by in the tree tops
Don't cry,
Don't you sigh.
For when the sand-man comes a steal-in
Un-der neath the sil-very moon.
I'll rock-a-by my ba-by
To dream land to a dream-y dream-y tune.

And rock-a-bye my ba-by to a Be-ta lulla-by
Rock-a-bye ba-by the sand-man is nigh
Rock-a-bye, rock-a-bye, rock-a-bye, ra-da
Shh...shh...ba-by's a-sleep.

You sang me to sleep, father
in that cushioned rocking chair
don't you remember, father,
how you gently stroked my hair.

I made you dinner,
soap and water with leftover spaghetti,

then you watched as I blew out my own candles,
and darkness swallowed me in one gentle breath,

on a blue plastic swing, higher and harder,
calloused hands lowering,
back-------and------forth,
in-------and------out,

a child's memories are built inside of teardrops
that fall,
like paint in water, smoke in air
dissolving into your blank stare.

Free Bird
A bird got caught in the house today
It would let out a little chirp of repetition
To send a resonance out
To see if anyone was on the same frequency
I felt it imperative to open at least one window for this bird
Whom was trapped in an unfamiliar place, sending out calls for help with no response,

As there was no one who understood or there was no one to listen

Realize, this is similar to the therapeutic relationship, in which, based on an already created structure, one must walk around and open whatever windows one can see or find, so that this person can get out of their structures of thought that keep them from experiencing life. Opening a window; opening as many windows as you can, will one day allow them to know where the windows are located. One day they will find them on their own.

Christine Marie
I am a mother, performance artist, real estate agent, and earth lover based out of Minnesota. I have been published twice in *Rock, Paper, Scissors* out of Hamline, and also in *Clean Sheets Magazine, The Edge Magazine,* and *Mason's Road*. I have also been a part of the Twin Cities Queer Voices Reading Series in 2011 and 2012.

The End of Thirst
Color me red
The jukebox said
To the dying night
As the moon drip slid
Down the whites of his eyes
Drop cloth breasts
To open thighs
And focused throat
No more she croaked
To blinking stars
His fingers pressed
Bulge to burst
The end of thirst

Supersonic Whisper
Because her date ended in rape
She never mentioned the hanging
Scent of rain
Under the winking crescent
Moon. Precarious
Moon.

Because her date ended in rape
She forgot the glass edge cling of red wine legs.
Futile climb.
Storm-tossed bouquet.
Helpless red swirl.

Because her date ended in rape
She forgot her tongue back's eager rise
To the occasion of salmon roasted walnut pate
Hapless tongue. Hopeless
Tongue.

There used to be permeability.
Her body ripe in opening
Orifices willing and celebratory.

The sound when she closed
Slipped between seconds at a dinner table miles away.
"What was that, Mommy?" the youngest daughter asked
at the whoosh and thump of vacuum suck

"What was what?" Mother replied
Eat your veggies, Dear."

Under the table, the family dog paused
Ears perked
Tail frozen
Breath held.

People Don't Want To Talk About Rape
People don't want to talk about rape.
They slip like wet noodles into short skirt talk and darting eyes.
This, you see, is easier
Than admitting that they too have holes,
Muscles that tire,
And a need to breathe.

I want to talk about rape
Because there is
A lot to say.

I want to say that ten years have passed and
On the motorcycle the other day the helmet strap pressed a certain way
Flew me through time and space and there I was
Wondering in a white lily sort of way
If this would be the last breath for which I fought.

Last month, my lover's kiss threatened to devour me
Her mouth pressed to mine
Sucked my soul through
'Till my cold sweat saved me.

People don't want to talk about rape.
They want to say we asked for it,
And I say,
Maybe.

Because when I watched from the ceiling
My soul stopped being a question
Came back to me
More solid than my body
Still today, every inhale celebrates survival
Every exhale, forgiveness.

What I reassembled
From my shattered self
Filters light in the loveliest ways
It shines off you and your reassemblies.
We are fourth dimension mosaic music
held together by gratitude.
Life not entitlement, but gift.

Daniel de C
Daniel de C is a writer, poet, and photographer. He is also a member of the Spanish Writers Association, Director of the *Gallo Tricolor Review*, and *Robespierre Review*. He's moving between California and Spain.

Daniel de C Poeta, escritor, pintor y fotógrafo, miembro fundador de la revista literaria Gallo Tricolor. Es miembro de la Asociación Colegial de Escritores de España. En la actualidad participa en espectáculos que funden poesía, música y teatro.

WHAT IF?
What if my name means Happiness?
I visit this place that you haven't already
Hating to see your great creative spirit
And your beautiful wife exhausted
Against the hard land of Past
Life and death on that side of the ridge
Into poor plastic graves
Where ifs and buts grow green
As the herbs do transforming ourselves
Looking at our bodies producing
A few bad and good flowers
With which do we exist
Do we form a whole with the Universe?
Knowing what's what
With one thing and another
Attempting to achieve the daily existence
And routines knowing what and what no
With the sun and the wind
Singing what next.

EXTINCTION OF THE PLANET
We laugh at first
Excerpt from a Journey of blood and tears
When Songs of Love and Maps of Freedom
Have undertaken to be revealed
And only are correspondences, notes
Quotes as wave lengths.
Sun rods into mountains
Hearing thrssh thrssh from the tress
Rotting nebulae.
Moon rides rivers
Just being able to pick and go
Objective characteristics
To the observance of geophysics.
Are we seeing our extinction?
Voices-- human crying
Voices-animal, voices-plant
But the Planet cannot sleep a wink
Bushing over the stream.
Voice-Life of Earth lives
And we laugh at first / Again. The same.

INFINITY TOUCH

Earth has one's fill of Infinity
Darkness, silence, cold
A heavy falling of feed on milk to and fro
At the base of the root of the trees
Having a finger in the pie
Playing stars through one's fingers
Saying to ourselves
All right. This is it
We're here
Searing beneath a dream
Finding that it is still
Soul with light
And more night remembering
That the infinity lies inside us
Thinking nothing
Singing everything alive:
"The Infinity
A cat that hasn't been touched
Flaming stars
On our straw roof.

Julie C
Julie C. received her B.A. in Anthropology and a M.A. in African American Studies from Georgia State University. She is currently completing her Ph.D. in World History with specialization in Africa and the Caribbean. Her commitment to colorism intends to raise consciousness, reconsider the internalization of white standards of beauty and initiate healing by presenting a new lens with which to see beauty and self-worth. The dissertation research grew out of her earlier graduate work on social constructs, concepts of whiteness and blackness and the formation of racial identities. Other research interests include imperial history, environmental history, race and ethnicity, social movements, traditional spirituality, and critical race theory. Aside from teaching World History, Julie spends her time traveling with her family, for personal and academic reasons, and broadening her culinary skills with exposure to other countries' delicacies. Her current hobbies include horseback riding and do-it-yourself renovation projects.

<u>My Great Escape</u>

The innocence and even the child was lost,
the morals and pleas for redemption were tossed,
the need to burn all the bridges I've crossed.

The blame was never mine to internalize,
it lies upon all of their shoulders to realize,
I was a friend, a lover & even a daughter that was victimized.

The changes that I have made to mask the guilt,
give power to the dominant structures society' has built;
My past looks like cloth pieces of an un-sewn quilt.

Each cloth square, a metaphorical memory tells of a story,
they show a wounded girl while you are smug with glory.
When we are judged for our sins, what will be your life's inventory?

Clinging to a prudent mannerism and a life of docility,
I've managed to counter all forms of virility and hostility;
threats of the past can no longer determine my fragility.

I recreated my stories and reinvented my self-worth,
yet I've run out of places to hide the memories on this earth.
I can no longer escape, it is time for my release, I need rebirth.

Its time for this emotional abuse to cease,
because whether you want me to or not,
I will heal my wounds & reclaim my peace!

--- JC, damaged but never broken ---

Tiffani D
My name is Tiffani and I'm a thriving survivor of sexual molestation. Living in Maryland, I'm given opportunities to use my experience as a tool to give others encouragement and support. I'm a firm believer that each of us has the strength inside to overcome any situation that comes our way. While being sexually molested in high school, I quickly realized that bad things happening life, and no matter how bad life may get, God is always there to help. It took me 12 years to overcome this struggle, but I made it and so can you.

<u>A Twelve Year Struggle</u>
As I sit reviewing over the years,
It seems like a life time ago when I shed those tears.
My heart and mind was scared with pain
It took me years to feel sane.
Your disgusting touches brought on anxiety and depression
Went to therapy to try to gain understanding and closure during session.
Therapy was helpful, but my tortured mind was still present.
I longed for a calm, peaceful world that I once saw as pleasant.
I remember trying to stay awake to stop the nightmares,
Most nights I thought no one cares.
I was soon a recluse,
Who thought, what's the use?
My innocent and loving world
Was now a repulsive and dreadful world.
Then one night I prayed as tears ran down my face,
Begging for comfort and to make my world a better place.
That night for the first time,
An arm wrapped around me and I knew I would be just fine.
As time went on
I realized I wasn't in the wrong.
The lies you told me,
Was your way of trying to keep me.
I broke through that chain
And gave God my pain
Many times I wished destruction on you,
But later was able to forgive you.
That was the first step in my healing process,
Now I'm a woman of success.
At times I'm triggered,
But my world doesn't become disfigured.
Looking back over the years,
It truly seems like a life time ago when I shed those tears.

Arika E
Arika E is a native of Nevada. She's been writing poetry since her early teens. She is the assistant poetry editor of *Helen: A Literary Magazine*. Some of her favorite writers and poets include James Baldwin, Lucille Clifton, Dorothy Parker, Langston Hughes, and Maya Angelou. Her work can be found in places like *300 Days of Sun, Burningword Literary Journal, Rockhurst Review, Gnarled Oak, Sippy Cup Magazine, Crab Fat Lit, Toasted Cheese, Open Road Review,* and *Blue Lyra Review*. When she's not writing or participating in poetry slams, she enjoys visiting museums, doing word searches, and watching old movies. She holds an associate's in Creative Writing and is working on her bachelor's in English from a university in Nevada.

Mother
Mother, Mother -
why did you let them
scar and disfigure me?
When you and father sent
me to Ghana, you didn't say
it was for vacation cutting. I
was stripped nude and held
down by three women with
hollow faces. A fourth held a
knife and tore away my flesh.
The blade ripped through my
vulva like tissue. I jerked my
body and screamed, but got
these icy words instead -
you silly girl.
Mother, Mother -
why did you let them
sever my joy? I have
no cleft between my legs
but sewn up memories of
what could've been. When
my fingers linger south,
there are no soft valleys,
but a jagged path of rocks
with no springs. My husband
has never seen me from the
waist down and I refuse to
let his sweet mouth nurture
what's ugly.
Mother, Mother -
I know why your soreness
is silent. It's the same one
subduing us in Sudan, Iran,
and Mali. You meant no harm
teaching me acts taught to you
as merciful. But now, I, swollen
with child, will raise one less
girl thinking her body is -
unclean.

Icy Hot

I walk around with a block
of ice in my belly with the
deftness of a figure skater.
But you'd never guess from
how charming I am that I'm
anything but warm. Under my
sleeves I've used my skin as a
cutting board and I've popped
more pills than the law should
allow. They keep me distanced
from the summer of '98. Family
told me since my cousin's mouth
wasn't a dick and *she* wasn't a *he,*
there was no crime. Three years
later when my father caught me
with the boy next door, he branded
me a slut for life.

Maybe if I had…
Why did I say anything?
Stupid…
always played in my head. And ice
chips that had formed from shame
crystallized into hate. What's a girl
to do when she's got the maturity of
a child, but the desires of a woman?
when the only trust exists in objects
that don't talk back? Every man who
I invited in my bed dropped cube
shaped promises – latching onto other
words, chilling in my veins, and
hardening my muscles. I don't need
their reminders of the person I am. All
I have to do is roll down my sleeves and *smile*.

Miranda E
My name is Maranda E. I am 23 years old. I was born and raised in Texas by a single mother. In 2004, my father was murdered by his girlfriend. I was only 11 years old at the time. A year later I lost my grandfather to cancer. Two years after that I lost my godfather to heart failure. My life became a never-ending tornado of pain as 10 years of my life was filled with depression, sexual abuse, painful love, and the emptiest feeling a girl can have. I was molested for almost two years beginning at age 13. At the time it was difficult for me to tell my mother or the police right away because I was afraid no one would believe me. When I was 16 years old, I was raped by a 25 year-old guy that I was dating. Since that day I have suffered from post-traumatic stress disorder during times of sexual intercourse and relationships. I wouldn't go to the police. Until I released my memoir, *Troubled*, only my two best friends were aware of my sexual abuse. It is now 2015 and I have come a long way. I have graduated with a BBA in Accounting from a university in Texas. I have begun my career in corporate Accounting. I am a student in an Business Graduate School at a university in southern Texas working towards my MBA with a concentration in Accounting. I am a self-published author and Founder of The Troubled Movement, an organization I created to use my story to uplift and empower young women who have faced life's adversities. In April 2014, I was baptized and I gave my life to God.

Silent Scream
My loudest scream was always silent
Born from a life of pain and violence
Absent to my surroundings while praying for guidance
The masks of smiles remain but inside I cried

As a victim I lost trust
I just learned to readjust
It was impossible to discuss
So when questioned I denied

Memories of my past begin to flow
About things my family will never know
Begging myself to let it go
As hard as I tried the pain never died

Tearing me apart inside and out
My mind filled with fear and doubt
Does anyone hear my silent shout?
Can anyone see behind my disguise?

Will life ever be normal again?
Will I continue to flinch when touched by men?
Will the truth ever go beyond this pen?
One day I will decide
To face my fears
To dry my tears
To share these years
And reveal the identity of the girl inside

The Phoenix
Like the Phoenix we disappear
Because the violent abuse we keep inside

Turns our shattered hearts cold

We forget who we are
Losing strength one day at a time
Looking for someone to trust

How can we explain trauma?
Will they believe the stories of sexual violence?
Labeled weak by the world

But we are strong survivors
Like the mythological bird representing true power
We triumph over life's adversities

We rise from the ashes
Created again but with no more pain
Given another chance at life

Jacquelyn F
Jacquelyn F lives in Illinois, is a Christian, single-mom with three young adult sons, as well as an educator, advocate, and aspiring author. She credits all the above for assisting her in the struggles faced as a survivor of childhood sexual abuse, as well as the joys that come with healing. She is very involved in her church community where she serves in several capacities. She also volunteers for two centers against sexual assault, is a member of the Rape, Abuse, and Incest National Network (RAINN) Speakers Bureau, and a member of a professional organization working to advance the status of women world-wide through advocacy and service. Throughout her healing process, art and writing have helped to bring meaning to the wide array of emotions experienced. In addition to the poems written here, she has written a children's book she hopes to one day publish.

LOSS OF HOPE
Who is this man they call death,
who feeds upon man's sorrow?
He lingers in the corners,
stirring up the echoes of our mind.
He permeates the daylight,
turns hope into fog.
Then, once there, he plants a seed;
pain helps it to grow.
Until at last, his job is done,
suffocating man's wish to be free.

THE SOLDIER
She's just a weary soldier
in life's battleground.

Searching, her war knows no bounds.
She battles not for glory.

She fights not for fame.
Yet, victory is her aim.

She years, struggles for her soul-
lost it years ago,
in strife which had no victor.

Now she continues onward
up the war-strewn path,
a fighter unto the last.

Some say she's brave and mighty; hear this, truth be told, for that she's oft uncertain.

Hark! Sound the war's battle cry; this she surely knows-memories are her foes.

Yet, with prayer- her battle song-
and her strength of heart, she does fight them as she must.

For lo, 'morrows round the bend,
There, she'll find her peace.
Her battle will rage no more.

Amber F

Forgiveness Is a Sin
I will never forgive
the man who slowly
unwound me through
several months toward
a climax I was
unaware of.

Each time we met,
he forced shadows
into my veins.

Only once did
I become aware that
he was trying to take me
to forbidden places.

When he took me
where no shadows
lurked when there
should have been,
 he taught me
men's intentions,
even over time,
can change when beauty
proves itself more
vulnerable than
a dandelion trapped
amidst a ferocious tornado,
and to this day, I wish
I did not have to know this.

Those Boys
I was told boys
do what they do because nine times out of ten
their harassment works. That one time
is apparently worth it for them among
the sinking sand of nine rejections they get.

I hate the fat guy leaning shirtless
against a telephone pole as he stares
me down while I walk home.
I hate the guy who crosses paths with me in
the middle of the road.

I especially hate those old men,
like the one who told me I was so pretty
I could be kidnapped. People tell me
I look sixteen, grandpa, so go screw yourself
with that cantaloupe you're cradling in your arms.

Trauma Treats the Brain Like Clay

Calloused fingers molded my
mind into the shape of a clay doll
scarred by fissures.

Trace your finger along
the fissures and remark
how closely they resemble your own.

It is true people's secrets are
buried deep within a kiln of clay;
secrets are insecurities.

They are not made of clay
but broken televisions, bruises,
torn-up cars, fractured glass.

She was accused
of harboring lovers like
the bruises from your lies.

You turned to me instead,
cheated on her, enfolded my
body in moist, gooey clay.

The clay melded into
my brain, and you shaped
it into broken televisions, bruises,
torn-up cars with fractured glass.

Though you never left me
bruised, you left deep welts on
my mind, now the density of clay,
easily moldable for any man's hands.

I may never quit writing about you.

Tafui F
Tafui F is a southwestern woman of Colorado. She is a doctoral candidate for a Doctorate of Philosophy in Humanities with a concentration in Africana Women's Studies at a university in Georgia. Her research interests include Black women's sexual agency, power, self-esteem, and wellness. Rav á Shelyn is an environmentalists working in the urban agriculture movement in southwest Georgia. She is interested in promoting the emotional, psychological, and physical benefits of community gardens. She is involved in the fight against sexual exploitation of women and children in Georgia. She holds writing and other artistic expressions as heal tool useful in achieving and maintaining a space of wellness.

Haiku: Those with Conceivably Inconceivable Dissonance
Rip flowers bleed
Voice lost beneath him
She don't know her name

Such a Sweet Little Girl
Raw sugar skin girl, caramelized
Hair that holds the fire of the sun
Her heart is ablaze
Since several tea cups of honey was taken
Robbed of her healing sweetness
There were sticky fingers in that house
Dripping with a golden blood elixir, stolen
Bones too frail with shame to testify
Sought definitions in eyes
Of those with larger bodies
With clearer articulated language
Those pillars of protection
Minds and sight developed
Yet, failed in that pivotal moment—that critical time to be heroic
Perception weak or unwillingly
Busy surviving in complicated locations
Searching for their own lost tea cups of honey
So long ago—Still—perhaps
Covering up their own hemorrhaging virgin blood that lingers
Silently remaining dismantled
By imprints of the sticky fingers

But then…. One day…Something new begun
Raw sugar skin girl, caramelized
Screamed her tears beyond the glare of the sun
. . . .

Find her now processing new honey
In her pastures of pleasure
Dancing the erotic in her ancient abyss

Tanka: for those refusing to be on the bottom of a sick food chain

Call on the rain
To restructure the insane
Hearts vessels strain
Yet its bruises remain
Know healing is not vain

Leslee Ann F

<u>Sitting On A Fence</u>
You were just a kid,
Just wanted to have fun...
Nothing else to do but play,
And get dirty in the sun...

Until one day,
Someone chose you to come out to play...
And all of a sudden,
You couldn't find the right words to say...

So there you're left,
While everyone else learns to be...

Was it the bounce in your step,
That set the flame in it's eyes to come your way...
Or was it all over your face,
And it came in and took it's place...

Now what left,
But the sudden passion to know...
Where it came from,
And why it went it places it shouldn't go...

11/9/98

VOID FELT...
MEMORIES SMELT...
LOSING HAND DEALT...

visions cloud... struggle to be proud... silent voices seemingly loud...

Subtle heart...
Numb from the start...
Identity torn apart...

Pushed Life...
Stabbed With A Knife...,
Obsessed With The Strife...

IN·THE·END
YOU·WILL ~~DESCEND~~ ASCEND
TO·A·PLACE·WHERE·YOU ~~COULD~~ CAN MEND

so that little girl you'll no longer have to defend...

LAF

... Circles will become full ... when you allow your heart to pull ....

... Pull away from the safe place you built ... break down all those walls of guilt ....

... Allow your passions to run free and wild ... realize that you're just a precious child ....

... Disguise the truth from everyone you know ... it's been your only safe place to go ....

... Pounding, pounding - slamming yourself down ... easier to smile, but too familiar is the frown ....

... Learn to battle from deep within ... put up your dukes and fight to win ....

... Pushing away everything that gets too close ... then God puts you here, different than most ....

... Now here you stand ... holding out your hand ....

... Offering solace and peace ... trying to help my demon cease ....

... Stop ... shhhh ... now listen to the pleasant sound ... allow yourself to feel the beauty that God's placed around ....

... "Things happen for a reason" I tend to say ... while still learning why God sent you my way ....

... My circle is rounding to become full ... with your help, winning is possible !!!!!!!!!!!
.... I thank God for you!!

L.A.F. 4-11-98

Jane G
When Jane G was 19, she told her mother that her stepfather had molested her during high school. The mother took *his* side, a betrayal that left Jane feeling lost and wracked with self-doubt. After years of floundering with identity and trust issues, Jane has forgiven her stepfather and mother and now lives in South Carolina with her husband and daughter. Therapy, good friends, and writing were her lifelines. Jane is a three-time Pushcart Prize Nominee and award-winning author. She is a firm believer that balance brings sanity. While writing a memoir (*Losing the* Dollhouse) that recounts the fallout of a family in turmoil, she made time to pen some light-hearted humor (*Flush This Book*). Without a good laugh now and then, we'd all need to be institutionalized. When she's not writing, she's editing other people's work and tutoring children. Her advice to other survivors of sexual abuse or assault: tell your story. You not alone.

A Letter to My Mother
For the record, I never intended to tell you what he did to me.
I knew you wouldn't, or couldn't, believe me.
Someone else told you while I was somewhere in the labyrinth of my soul
creating new places to hide.
You were always away when he did it—and he waited us both out.
I remember a Sunday afternoon in winter while you were at choir practice.
On my stomach with head propped up on elbows, I read The Scarlet Letter
until my eyes surrendered to a nap,
face down on the open pages, black hair fanning out over my cheeks like a blanket.
My stepfather was stealthy.
In the haze of slumber I couldn't see his droopy middle-aged face.
His six-foot-two frame straddled the small of my back.
His silence was startling. No explanation. Only movement.
His weight pressed into me just enough to make it harder to breathe.
His hands crept under the edges of my David Bowie T-shirt,
fingers gently tugging at the elastic of my bra and unhooking it.
A stiff iciness seeped into me, like some glacier sweeping over every muscle,
painful and cold until my bones hurt.
I lay there, not breathing, hoping he would get up, change his mind, leave, anything else.
*Please Mom, come home this time, come home right now—see one of these
strange and quiet confrontations...*
This prayer was never answered.
He dug his thumbs into the skin of my back in steady, deliberate circles,
outward toward my armpits and then around to my back and breasts.
My stomach, empty and raw, churned the bile until it rose in my throat, threatening—
just enough for me to taste how I felt:
Vomit.
I pressed up with an urgency that startled him enough to lose his balance.
He was still on his knees as I scrambled to my feet.
And for a brief moment I was taller than he was.
As I turned to leave the room he grabbed the hem of my thin blue cotton skirt,
clutching it in his fist like a child.
"Stay, stay," he whimpered, "I need you. I just want to rub your back."
"I have to go upstairs," was all I could manage.
My mouth still tasted like vomit, and
I could feel my breasts hanging loosely against my unfastened bra.

Erika G
Erika G is a mother, daughter, sister, friend, and colleague. She resides in Texas. She considers herself a leader, a servant, an encourager, flawed and enough. She's worked in the live events industry for over 15 years. Taking on leadership roles professionally and being a single mother continues to teach her that she still has a lot to learn. However, she quickly had to learn how to think outside of the box when faced with challenges, to realize the importance of asking for help when needed, and to understand that we may not be able to control our circumstances but our attitude plays a key role in our outcome. Erika enjoys reading, working out, journaling, spending time with family, and attending sporting events. In some of the toughest moments in Erika's life, people, events, and resources were the key to encouraging her to persevere. She has often heard people say that "hurt people, hurt people." In her thirties, she decided to take a step of faith to face some of her deepest fears so that healing could take place. She believes if one person would take that step then the cycle can change to "healed people, helping people heal."

Free Indeed
Darkness surrounded the little girl as she experienced so much pain. She often thought if the abuse didn't stop that she would go insane.
She tried to give her mom a clue as she cried and wrapped her arms around her mother's knee. However, her mother did not understand the clues and did not know what she could not see.
Each time she experienced the abuse her hope slowly slipped away. She often thought life would be better if only she could escape.
She did what she thought was best and buried all the pain. She was convinced that was the way to cope and the only way to stay sane.
Years past and what she realized is what she thought helped her cope only but a mask on the pain. Over time the internal pain grew stronger and she knew things had to change.
One night she cried out "Lord, the pain is overwhelming and I need you so much! Father, do you hear me? I need your healing touch!"
As tears filled her eyes that night and her heart overflowed with pain, God touched her with his love and her life slowly began to change.
She knew that night she was in bondage but soon she would be free because God promised that "whom he sets free will be free indeed!"

Hold On
It seems dark now but the light will eventually shine.
It seems confusing now but I promise it will make sense after a while.
It seems like you're alone but there are so many people that can relate.
It seems hopeless today but God will not give you more than you can take.
It is painful today but I promise the pain will eventually ease.
The storm is raging but it will eventually end and you will experience His peace.
Today, your tears are symbolic for your pain and sorrow.
Eventually, they will be symbolic for your freedom and hope for tomorrow.
"Depression", "Pain", "Hopelessness," are engraved in your heart today.
"Freedom", "Joy", "Peace" will soon snag their place.
Hold on! Don't give up! God's word says "weeping may endure for a night but joy will come in the morning."
Hold on! Don't give up! He's a man that will fulfill all of his promises.

Is It Possible

Is it possible to spend years without a clue?
Is it possible for something so dreadful to happen to me or you?
Is it possible for past memories to resurface in a day?
Is it possible to discover the truth and keep living the same way?
Is it possible to go from bondage to finally being set free?
Is it possible the abuser took advantage of more than you and me?
Is it possible we have been making decisions from our childhood pain?
Is it possible for good to come from years of hidden shame?
Is it possible to learn to love and appreciate the person who God created us to be?
Is it possible in the midst of darkness there is light we cannot see?
There are so many questions that surface as we journey down the healing path. We may never know the answers but realize the questions are "normal" to ask.

Arden H

Arden H is an all-around queer who grew up dodging alligators in Southern Louisiana. Ze holds a BA from a college in Massachusetts, an MFA in poetry from a university in Virginia and is, at present, a PhD student in Creative Writing at a university in Nebraska where ze is an Assistant Poetry Editor for *Prairie Schooner*. Arden's poetry has appeared in journals such as *Willow Springs, Joslyn NOW, and Cripping Femme*. Ze won first place in the Gaffney/ Academy of American Poets contest in 2013 and was runner up for the Gertrude Claytor Prize in Poetry in 2006. While primarily a poet, Arden's publications include, a piece of creative non-fiction in *Western Humanities Review* and a fairy tale in the anthology *Women's Work*. In 2008, Arden was a poetry fellow at the Lambda Literary Retreat for Emerging Writers. Ze is working on a fictionalized memoir told in poems that delves into adoption, race, gender, sexuality, and disability.

Missing the Slap by Seven Months
Karen said, *bullet dodged*. This is only partially true.
What didn't split bone passed through. The almost clean
entry/exit wound carried my blood to the wall where splatter sticks
and I have to remind myself that I am not brick, not stucco
not the cornerstone where metal is lodged.
       Karen said *dodged* like it was something more than luck,
       as if I'd had the sense to duck and cover when I'd
       been ducking friends' questions covering the ass of a lover
       who'd cross arms over my car keys, pocket my wallet, and settle
       weight into boots, back blocking the door till I forget
       the back stairs and that I shouldn't have to say *no* so many times.
       Repetition transforms *no* to *I know you're having a rough day.*
              No, you don't have to apologize anymore.
              I know there's no one who loves me more.

Discredited
I fled for my flesh but not my life
after the fist she said she'd hold back fell.
Danger's discredited when we survive.

The truth turns slanted when we tell.
And the truth is: I don't know if I was believed
after the fist she said she'd hold back fell.

I told and to follow speaking grieved.
The moral's not learned until the end.
And the truth is: I don't know. If I was believed

stopped mattering. There were needs to tend
poems or bread and bills to pay.
The moral's not learned until the end

when it can't be written any other way,
and nothing I found was what I thought I'd make.
Poems or bread? And bills to pay

arrive in every violent action's wake.
I fled for my flesh but not my life
and nothing I found was what I thought I'd make.
Danger's discredited when we survive.

<u>Megaera</u>
The bruise did not feel safe enough to say
a word in bed after she found my throat.
Blood waited until I drove away

through Boston's dingy dawn. That day
I spent silent and clenching while I wrote
the bruise did not feel safe enough to say

that terror commandeered the play.
Unfolding in secret script I couldn't note,
blood waited until I drove away

to well beneath my skin then slip the fray
and coil behind the bed rail rope.
The bruise did not feel safe enough to say

much in deference to her jealous way
which coagulated under all it did not coat.
Blood waited. Until I drove away,

I did not realize what had been betrayed
or what would linger in an urn with hope.
The bruise did not feel safe enough to say.
Blood waited until I drove away.

Robin H
Robin H is a sporadic blogger for the *Huffington Post*, a full-time mom and president of a communication and marketing firm. She's currently finishing a young adult novel, "The Call of the Weird," about adolescent awkwardness and the need to be true to who you are.
Robin lives in New Jersey.

For the daughter of my rapist
I see my rapist on Facebook.
You stand beside him, statuesque but stiff.
The daughter who fills him with pride.
His right cheek raised in a smile
Gently holding your waist as his blue rugby shirt and faded jeans droop.

Your sequined, strapless gown hugs your youthful curves.
The green grass rimmed by clean, silver rocks you stand on as false as your French tips and blonde highlights.
Beneath the thick mascara and newly waxed brows, your eyes are black pools soulful and searching for more.
They scream of the hope and joy I remember once pulsing through me, now just an echo.
But in your eyes, I see it and I remember.
Never lose that light, beautiful girl.
It's what is real.
It's what keeps you full.

I Want My Little Girl Back
I want my little girl back.
The one with the shaggy brown hair.
Who amazed her big brother's friends with her slap shot in street hockey
Who built forts made from branches and unearthed worms in the Connecticut woods with her cousin Stu
Who sat alone in the basement for hours, reading the lyrics from Jim Croce's "You Don't Mess Around with Jim" as the album played, feeling every word to every song
Who dreamed big – of living in a Malibu beach house and being a guest on "The Tonight Show"
She left me at 19.
She left me as I lie in a stranger's unmade bed with the door wide open.
She left me as I felt his penis plunge so far and deep I thought my insides would rip.
They did.
And I did.
My spark gone, replaced with need.
The need to walk, not run
The need to fill an empty cup
The need to listen to others because I can't be sure
Of anything, anytime, anymore.
She was sure.
She is no more.
Forty years is a long time to linger, but the spark can become a fire still.
With love for a spirit long lost and for others young and old, she'll grow.
Into a blaze that's not the same
But with a warmth that inspires us all.

Angela K
Angela was awarded the Ellen Taliaferro Scholarship for Domestic Violence and Abuse to attend the 2010 San Francisco Writers Conference and performed for BAWAR at Lake Merrit. Angela published her memoir, *Lupin*, in 2013 and speaks regularly for SHARP, an army wide rape and sexual assault program. She was the featured speakers bureau member in the RAINN newsletter for National Runaway Awareness month 2013 and currently supports artistic expression and healing through music and art. She also posts articles about domestic violence and rape on the Lupin House Facebook page. Angela believes that healing from rape and domestic violence is possible and that music can be a very powerful tool to recovery and ultimate forgiveness.

Raise the Dead
You thought you could take a flower
And shake all the leaves from it
And by shear force of your power
It would wither and submit

You took the lion from my soul
And turned her into a lamb
You took away my control
You took away who I am

But I will rise up from the dead
Where you left me in this hell
And I will take the dead up with me

I will rise up from the dead
We'll have our stories and we'll tell
I will take them all up with me
I will raise the dead

I'm not sitting in my room
Letting time fill up the space
I'm not dwelling on the pain
I am only taking back my grace

You did not get away
Taking all your broken hearts
Where you thought that it had ended
I will tell you that it starts

I will rise up from the dead
Where you left me in this hell
And I will take the dead up with me
I will rise up from the dead
We'll have our stories and we'll tell
I will take them all up with me
I will raise the dead

You can not take my life away
You will not cause me to crumble
I will survive, I will not sway
You will not cause me to stumble

I will rise up from the dead
Where you left me in this hell
And I will take the dead up with me
I will rise up from the dead
We'll have our stories and we'll tell
I will take them all up with me
I will raise the dead
I will raise the dead

<u>Revelation of a Flower</u>
What makes a flower beautiful?
Does the sun have to shine?
Does the breeze toss it gently?
Do the insects come to dine?
Does the scent spread cross the field?
Yet it is humble in Gods eyes?
Standing totally revealed,
Simplicity defied.

Because without a sound,
Just by rising from the ground,
By choosing to stay open,
A flower is profound.
And that is why it strikes us,
So beautiful each day,
It is not so simple,
to everyone's dismay.

Chong K

Chong K is an Asian-American survivor of human trafficking and child sex exploitation. Ms. K was born in South Korea and became a citizen in the United States in 1984 through the State of Oklahoma. In 1994, Ms. K met a guy who was disguised as her boyfriend, but instead was abducted and sold into slavery in various parts of Northern Nevada and other areas within the US borders still unknown to her. Through the abuse and psychological damage that occurred during her experience of trafficking, she learned the only way to survival was to rank up in the organization to find a way to escape. Attempted escape meant torture or death, having witnessed the punishment of traffickers for years, so when she sensed her chance, she finally successfully escaped in 1997. Chong began a life on the run, of terrified survival… drugs, prostitution, petty crimes on the street.

Between 2003-2007 she reinvented herself; Chong first volunteered her time as a legal advocate through domestic violence court programs. Today, as a recognized survivor of human trafficking having her story told in the movie *Abduction of Eden* (2013), she has devoted her life to promoting human and civil rights through public speaking, FBI and police training and as an outspoken advocate for countless victims. She uses her personal story to enlighten NGOs and political officials and organizations with the goal of strengthening the advocacy system to effectively reach and assist victims of trafficking. Chong K has appeared on several news networks: CNBC, CNN, and International BBC, talk shows such as Montell and numerous local radio and television stations.

<u>Skin Deep</u>
What is it you say?
You want me?

Your claim of racism is delusive
Because you care for me?

Tell me your description,
Paint a picture of me,
What illusion do you represent,
As you eloquently say?

You speak of my robust bottoms?
Utilizing the stereotypes of my ethnicity
magazine which only misrepresent sexual lust you deem to see?

Do you see past between my thighs
And see the story in my brown eyes?

How about my long black hair?
Or do you imagine me in such degrading fashion.

My almond shaped eyes, my foreign accent from my ancestors lips,
Do you even hear the words I'm saying to you?

Wanting to wrap your hand around my neck with your darkest insecurities with the "Love me long time" you classify?

How about my history past of my Native skin, do you dare to taint it with one more lie?
Maybe to you it's harmless, but have you once gotten to know me?

Aside from my female anatomy?
My skin that you so savagely want to take apart, yet you don't know why?

Fetish you say?
Ha! Now you're talking, yes speak words of truth.

You see I am on to you and your
Arrogant invitation,
It is not the "like" that you have in me,
But the entitlement that you feel you can own me.

How can you say you want to be my King, when you know nothing about this Queen?

I am more than a flesh, or an ethnic of your standards, I am more than just color stereotype you chose to conceive.

I am a heartbeat that is earned, an intimacy that is worth the wait & most of all I am a vessel that can not be broken by unclean hands.

Please . . I can not hear no more.
Save the lines to someone who is desperately wanting to be spoon-fed with these affliction.

In the beginning, you never saw me.

Stage It
Life is not missed, opportunity is.
When you have little patience of what's to be next,
Gamble your chance into hope.
While gossip your words into prayer.
Raise your inspirers into empowerment and
stress yourself into the mindset of "It's mine."

Remember NO ONE can do it for you.
Believe that you deserve the spotline to shine.
Make every moment your only audition,
No matter what may come,
Don't intoxicate yourself with negativity,
Break up with insecurity
And leave room for ambitions.

Utilize fear to guide you into different paths,
Instead of consuming you.
Be thrivers not takers.
What you have taken from someone will be taken from you.
Things were meant to be left behind.
Treasures are for passing on
And Legends always remain.
Choose what you want right now.
It starts, today.

Ignorance is Bliss
As I walk in the door
I can feel the eyes sizing me up.
I walk in with a limp
I'm immediately discriminated.
By the whispers of talk,
Moving away from my presence
As if you have the right
To cast me aside.

I do not hold no trophies
Or was handed expensive bread
To fulfill an empire,
Yet everything I earned
I started from scratch.
You see, I was a high school dropout
not cause I wanted to be,
after constant bullying and racial discrimination
my mind said, "no more."

Shortly after that I didn't realize running away
Came with a price tag,
As long as I fell in the system,
My name would later transfer to the human trade.
Exploiters just eagerly waiting to rape my soul away.
Breaking me down to where my mind would leave me
In a pathos of insanity.

All shatter pieces on the ground,
Came to America to find my way out of poverty
"Land of the Free" is the sign given to thee,
But how many slaves must suffer from lies like these?

The government promises justice, are they so blind
Or maybe it's just plain ignorance on their part
We know corruption is what makes the market go round and round.
The economy is crashing and yet blame is cast on both side of political pole
Yet we are still undiscerning to what WE want to believe.

A sea of naive children relying on media to educate their perception,
Yet so many find fascinating when we are taught
The only way to get to the top is desperation,
While Satan awaits on the other end.

Don't you see the ultimate cause of this atrocity is that our children
Are basically crying out . . .
"I just need you with me."
So many films exploit or glamorize the pornography
Of our children,

While we watch films of sorcery and magic
To take us to Never land,

Keep us in the bubble we don't want to hear the truth,
And while we are in it,
Where have our children disappeared to?

I'm called constantly by the people in power
To "help" them educate the public so they
Receive a "Star" on their platform while
Confessing my horrific testimony,
I get a tissue and a simple "Thank you" with no sincerity insight.

My words have become their stats,
Yet it's tweaked to their likings,
Many of us who share our names
Are always ignored,
Just like the slaves who built the White House of America,
Are their names ever memorialized? No.

I never went to college,
But what my experience taught me you will never
Find in any institute or entity anywhere.
I couldn't find my way through HS Geography,
But my hustling navigation taught me
The exact points of sellers and buyers.

I wasn't a mathematician, since
I failed that stereotype of being "Asian-American"
But I learned how to "hustle"
My way through Poverty Pimping,
When I decided to be the "Bottom Bitch"
of Uncle Sam.

I got my education in Political Science,
When I met my "trick" who happen to represent
A state that I once lived in,
After being the puppet for a show he paid for,
I learned that there was way to get rid of the score.

And last but not least, economy is what I learned more
About this trade, you can't do any of the above if you
Have no concept of the world economy in your hands.
From trade to distribution, to money laundering and racketeering
From drugs to human exploitation
All of that with no education.

So, if you think being wealthy equals to intelligence . . .
Think again, before you head down that path.
Social Status may open some doors,
But the streets open so much more,
But be cautious in your path
Everything we learn comes with a price.

Toby K
Toby K is a recent high school graduate who will be attending a university in Indiana in the fall 2015 to pursue studies in neuropsychology. In her free time, she enjoys volunteering, working out and reading.

Harvest me
From a barren land.
Take me to
Where I cannot stand.

Use the big tractor,
As simple hands won't do.
Harvest me *please*,
Just take me away from you.

I'm tough to uproot,
That much I know.
But you managed to get me,
I have the scars to show.

I'm strong in a field,
I can stand tall.
But you corned me when I was alone,
And acted surprised after my fall.

We're made of straw,
Not steel.
But that doesn't stop the pain
From being all too real.

You were my best friend,
I'd told you of my escape.
Nowhere in that plan,
Did I include rape.

A selfish act
From a little straw boy
Who didn't care
About the life he'd destroy.

So let the strong winds blow,
Let the rain come crashing down.
Because this time it'll be **you**
Who in my tears will drown.

***

I was asked to write about
the things one can never say aloud.
I was asked to write about
this toxic hovering cloud.

The words I'm supposed to say
are the ones in my heart I feel.
The words I'm supposed to say
are the ones unfortunately all too real.

I'm required to write stanzas
about aching and beautiful truth.
I'm required to write stanzas
about the boy who stole from me my youth.

"Make an illusion" my teacher tells me,
so I'll allude to this life changing mistake.
"Make an illusion" my teacher tells me,
so I'll allude to the worst of hearts--heartbreak.

The assignment says to focus on a moment,
yet my "moment" has become my life.
The assignment says to focus on a moment,
yet my moment cuts through paper like a knife.

I am asked to write a poem,
so I'll put words into a shape.
I am asked to write a poem,
so I'll talk whisper about rape.

I've been asked to bear my heart,
and here upon a page it lies.
I've been asked to bear my heart,
for my heart is the only truth in a sea of lies.

This is the last stanza,
of a poem too dark to write.
This is the last stanza,
of a story that almost never came to light.

Diane L
Diane L is a graduate student in Expressive Arts Therapy at a university in Massachusetts. She is a longtime advocate of people who have lived experienced domestic and sexual violence, child abuse and neglect and addictions. Educated as an early childhood teacher, Diane has incorporated her teaching philosophy and skills into her work as a self-defined therapeutic educator. Diane is an artist, proud aunt, dedicated worker and loyal friend. She is active in group work focused on trauma recovery in the New Hampshire area. Diane is a survivor of gang rape as a teen and sexual assault as an adult. She has been in recovery from addiction since 2001.

Interested
I don't need or want you to fix me. I know I have worth until you give me advice to fix me.
I don't need or want you to treat me as if I'm damaged or fragile. I have strength until you act for me.
I don't need you to judge me or be impatient. I am my own worst critic and I am frustrated.
I don't need you to tell me when I do something wrong, I know I am fallible and sometimes my actions hurt others.
I am not dangerous to you or anyone else. I am most at risk to myself.
I don't need to feel better about myself by bringing you down. When you reciprocate I feel capable. When you ask me to compromise or minimize myself, I learn to be small, silent, and invisible.
I am depressed not because of you but because I'm sad, angry, jealous, afraid and I can't express it. This is not intentional, willful or about you. Your defensiveness isn't helpful.
I don't need you to take care of me. I am taking care of myself even if you don't understand it or agree with my choices.
I believe you are the expert on yourself. Trust that I know myself and my feelings, thoughts and actions more intimately than you.
When you don't or won't, I don't trust my own experiences.
I am interested in knowing when I've hurt you, so I can change.
I am interested in feeling your acceptance and love in the ways you can offer it knowing that others can meet my needs in ways you aren't able to.
I am interested in sharing ideas and hope to better our communication and relationship in direct, clear and timely ways.
I am interested in forgiveness of myself and others.
I am interested in safe touch and comfort.
I am interested in being seen and heard.
I am interested in safety, yours and mine.
I am interested in trusting me and you
I am interested in loving myself and you even when it is messy and complicated.
I am interested in sharing this journey with you.

Body
My body is a crime scene.
Bloody, broken, violent.
My body is a war zone.
Destroyed, damaged, angry, dead.
My body is a virus.
Contagious, toxic, must be eradicated, quarantined.
My body is a famine.
Empty, lacking, starving.
My body is a collapsed mine.
Dark, cold, suffocating.
My body is a fire.
Mottled, raging, deceptive, reeks.

My body is a bomb.
Unreliable, unpredictable, weapon of mass destruction.
My body is an invitation.
Ridicule, shame, abuse, disease, guilt.
My body is a report card.
Failure, does not work well with others, needs improvement,
Poor conduct, resistant.
My body is a trap.
Enticing, sneaky, malicious, maiming.
My body is a cage.
Locked, rusted, permanent.
"Do Not Feed the Animal."

<u>The Journey Home</u>
What happens when the advocate, the helper and the healer becomes the victim?
You would think she would recognize the signs,
Be certain what has happened and know exactly what to do next.
You wouldn't think she'd feel shame about telling her family, the police or friends.
She is no different though or better armed against the stain of rape.
She is scared, worried, confused, angry, disappointed.
Feels unsafe, dirty, damaged, alone and ugly.
All the words, a salve she offered her clients, seem empty, wrong and dishonest.

He stole her safety, her power, her love of her body.
He robbed her of the esteem she felt bearing witness to others who have gone before her.
He ignited a civil war in her brain and her heart, long after his hands left her body.
His smell and touch linger for hours, days, weeks.
His voice louder than hers runs constantly in tapes that loop through her brain.

She fights him in her dreams, in the shower, with her lover in a most valiant effort.
She feels him creep back into her bed, hears his whispers, feels his hands.
Knowing that it is not happening now is hardly a comfort. Insanity.
On the edge of falling onto sleep, she is rattled alert.
Eyes spring open. Heart racing. Drenched in sweat. Breath catches. Dying.
The room spirals into focus in the bright, constant lamplight.
She slowly moves her fingers, her legs, and her hands.
She is not paralyzed.
Somewhere between fear and relief, she recalls all those who care about her.

There are solutions. Medications have worked. Crisis lines offer brief respite.
Writing and drawing have offered relief at times.
In the aloneness, she is curious about how many other women are
Lying awake, scared, alone and ashamed in their own beds.
She's met them. She knows they're out there.
It seems sad to belong to a club with such vast membership,
Such high dues, and do little connection.
She is certain the rapist sleeps soundly,
The benefits of membership in his club are never challenged.

In the morning, she enters the day with energy or caution,
Depending on how late he kept her up.
She enjoys going to work and there is power in numbers in the daylight.

She is surrounded by people who won't criticize, make careless remarks or
Blame the victim. There's a certain safety in that.
She listens to client stories and when her heart is stirred she silently chants,
"Yes. I know. I am a survivor, too. The wounds do fill in and heal."
The healing happens in the presence of others. Her voice becomes stronger and clearer.
Joy seeps back into her life through survivors growing, learning and
Celebrating life together. The wound is healed.

Diamante L
Diamante L has been in love with reading since she was a child. She spent many hours listening to her mother read to her when she was young. As she grew older, she enjoyed reading novels of all genres: horror, fantasy and some romance to name a few. She began writing in college and published some poetry in anthologies over the years. After her kids were older, she wrote as a form of self-expression and decided she wanted to share her stories with others. Most of her writing is very personal and stems from her own experiences and those of her family and friends. She writes to encourage hope and possibility to those who read her stories. Diamante believes that everyone should try to leave their own positive mark in the world, to make it a better place for all. Writing is the way that she is attempting to leave her mark—one story at a time.

Life
From the dust we are made,
To the dust we return;

In the days of our lives,
Many lessons are learned;

To believe is a key,
To take risks is a cost;

To feel true joy and peace,
We must understand loss;

Life is indeed a game,
That we must play with care;

And its greatest achievement,
Is the love that we share.

The Dance Of Life
Life is a dance; it is a dance
Of love, of compassion,
Of nature, of wit,
If you do it right.

A dance
Of happiness, of holiness,
Of peace, of helpfulness,
If you follow your own enlightened path.
And when your last days come,
You will know if you've succeeded
By the people who have gathered around you
And the people who hold you in their hearts.

For life is not a game of chance;
It is a testament
Of who you are as a person
And who you have become,

Through the path
You have chosen to walk
While you found yourself
Here on earth.

Don't Give Up
When you've tried your best,
Been challenged and tested,
And you're still wading through the muck,
Don't give up.

When your dreams aren't handed,
To you on a silver platter,
And you feel like nothing matters,
Don't give up.

When others tell you
How wonderful their lives are,
Know that they too have scars.
Don't give up.
When sorrow hangs around,
Like a thorny crown,
And everybody tells you to smile,
Don't give up.

Life is a series of tests
And tribulations
With an occasional vacation, so
Don't give up.

The sun always shines,
After it's been gone a while,
Know you'll make it through your trials.
Don't give up.

For others are watching you,
To see what you will do.
And if they see you make it through,
They might not give up.

Jannina L
My name is Jannina Marie L and I am 23 years old. I was born and raised in New York. I am a survivor of childhood sexual abuse and teenage rape. I became an advocate for sexual abuse and rape awareness in 2011 and became a RAINN Speakers Bureau member in 2012. I am in my last year in college pursuing a Nursing degree as well as actively planning my wedding in 2017.

<u>In silence</u>
The cobwebs stick.
The memories slip
Past walls
Of dammed emotions.
In my eyes
Look close
You'll find the embers
Of a hope still burning,
Still yearning
To be set ablaze.
Hope
Slides on glass
Tripping fast
The feet of the woman
Growing.
Breaking free
Trying to be
The other side
Of the coin
She was
Forcefully dealt.
Regaining strength
Through breaths that
Exhale the old
And bring on the new
She fights
Like the rising moon
To be
Who she was meant
To be.
To fight
The black stamps on her
Canvas
Making them part
Of the
Masterpiece
Rather than
Shaming them
Under layers
Of paint.

<u>Year 20</u>
Identity,
Formed,

Not discovered.
Truth,
So ruthlessly
Forced upon.

Eyes open
To
The dark
After
Searching
All your life
For the light.

Hands reach
And find
The slippery
Cracks
Of a broken
Wall.

There is no
Lighthouse.

Hope falls
In the crook
Of life's smile.
And in a way you always knew it would.

A call to forgiveness
And a higher
Calling
Shape your heart into
A question
Mark
Of
Struggled
Understanding
And you develop
Your divine
Armor.

Words slide off
And you are
Immune.

Immunity.
To
What and to whom is unknown.
But you
Feel
Protected.
And for now,

That's all that matters.

Knowledge
Only lies
In what door
You chose to open,
And those forced
Open by
The winds
Of reality and
Accidental
Awakening.

The
Future
Sounds as foreign
As a sci-fi
Novel
And you step forward
Hoping only for
The next second
Of clarity
And you inhale.

Inhale.
Breathing in the peace
Exhaling out
The rotten,
The broken,
The lost.

Year 20.
Lost yourself
Found yourself
Saved yourself.

A process,
A mountain
A molehill
Of which you
Can take credit
Only for
Reaching for
The lifeboat.

LOOK UP.
Look up.
Look up
And see.
And witness.
And feel
What you were searching for.

What you were longing for.
What was yours for the taking.

He Lives.
Christ Jesus Lives.
Salvation to impart,
You ask me how I know
He lives,
Well,
He lives within, my heart.

<u>Nightmares</u>
Kisses from the underground
Caresses from the snake
Blending realms of consciousness
A frightened girl awakes.

Fight against the fear
The panic and the pain,
Reality offers comfort
In sleep the dark remains.

Awake, and taste the morning
Erase the past of sleep.
Although like cobwebs clinging
The memories stay deep.

Marie Louise
Marie Louise lives in Sydney. Founder of Evolve Yourself Institute. Author, *Discover Worlds Within*

I am passionate about sharing tools, strategies, education and inspiration to as many people on this planet all over the world to live a life of love, passion, peace and in a space of possibility and personal potential. I have dug deep into the me I perceived myself to be, chopped away at unconscious conditionings and beliefs, knocked down walls of silent self sabotage, healed this body of past trauma and opened myself up to unconscious fears. Realising my thoughts could sometimes be my best entertainment, I became my own observer of the regular stand up gig, my mind would be presenting, Reconnected to my sensory body and practiced watching my emotions. With the personal fascination of human behaviour, intrigue into the workings of the brain and experiential realisations, my world opened up to live a life of love, spontaneity, joy and expansion as my constant. I have previously owned my own drilling company and spent 22 years in the mining industry. I have been a mother, daughter, lover, wife, friend and business owner. This simple life has made it possible for me to share things, simply. Life isn't as serious as we think and we have the power to create the life we choose, irrelevant of our life beginnings. To be responsible for ourselves and become aware of our own evolution will expose a collective transformation and making conscious choices is where possibility of global peace exists. Education, Experience and Expansion is the power of the people for awareness of evolution and waking up to greatness.

<u>the fuel of fear, finds the sun</u>
With the mask of my face
I dance with disgrace
that freezes my moves and motions
In the break of the day
when there should be play
the shadow of the sun exposed darkness
as I played with finesse
in my pink little dress
to the beat that I knew
where cobwebs grew
The prison of my past
held me bound in my heart
and the shackles of shame
exposed my new game
As I take a deep breath
I see the warmth in my chest
and with that big sigh
I look up to the sky
As the world that was mine
had frozen in time
I find that fear as the fuel
that finally freed me
with the fire that now flames
where love shows no pains
with a new dance that now flows
in all grace that it shows
I wake up to the power
that resides within me
that takes me on a journey
the more I see
Forever grateful for the fuel that freed me.

Sherese M
My name is Sherese M, and I am a call center supervisor. I am from Texas by way of Illinois. I am a proud mother of three young adults. I have been writing poetry and prose since my teenage years for the very reason this book exists, to heal. I began reciting later in my adult years. I have performed in the College of Lake County's Fear No Art Festival and have been published in the College of Lake County's "Prairie Voice," 2006 edition. I was the resident poet for the Valarie Alpert Dance Company and performed in the production of Between Skin, October 2007. I also co-hosted an open mic night at comedian Juz Jokkin' Comedy Club in Illinois. My goal in life is to continue to be an example of perseverance and to become more accomplished as a writer. I hope my selections provide strength to the mind, body, and soul.

You Stole from Me
You stole from me.
You stole my innocence
or what was left.
Either way,
It did not belong to you.

You stole from me.
All that, at the time,
seemed precious and good to me.

My sense of belonging in the world,
Pride of self.
You stole from me.

Only that moment.
Because I dare not let you steal another.
Find comfort in that moment, if you dare.

Because I say, NEVER, not again!

Never Again
You can't take what was never yours.
I said
You can't take what was never yours,
Like my soul, my joy.
Something you tried to destroy.

My muse won't let you,
My spirit won't let you,
Hell
My family and friends won't let you.

You may have been successful in the past
But your days of harvesting souls won't last.
Because you can't take what was never yours.

You may think you can walk through walls and closed doors
But you can't take what was never yours.

My spirit knows the devil is a liar.
He's not the seller of souls, he's a buyer.

I will remain standing as your soul burns in hell's fire.
Because my God is an awesome God.

He will cater to my every desire
And I will sing his praises like the town crier.

As I scream to the top of my lungs, my belly full of fire.

You can't take what was never yours.

Kio M

My name is Kio and I am a survivor of sexual violence. I am a branch administrator for a staffing company, but my goal is to become a productions assistant so I can get my foot in the door to accomplish my dream--which is to become an actress. Of course I would love to play featuring roles and lead roles, but would definitely play an extra... as long as it has to do with acting, I'm okay with it! In my roles, I want to play someone who is strong and confident in everything because if you don't have confidence in what you are going for, there will be no point in pursuing your dream. The message I want to put out there is no matter the color of your skin or the life you used to live, you can always be whatever you want if you speak it, believe it and take the steps to receive it.

Untitled

I've been lost and in the dark, it felt like there was no light. I didn't know what was wrong and I didn't know what was right, well at least that's what it felt like. I didn't know who to turn to, I felt so used and confused I didn't know what to do and, not realizing God is a privilege only giving Him attention every other weekend. But then everything started going wrong for me. I was so blind I still don't understand how I could not see. I was searching for love and peace, but I guess then I was sleep. I prayed every night that my soul would be the soul that my Father would keep. My judgment was so clouded back then, I didn't realize that I was going towards the deep end. I know now that I am restored because my Savior died for my sins. I look at Him not only as my Father, but also as my best friend. He had a choice and that choice was me. God I rejoice everyday because You are my King! With Your love Your blessings and Your touch, I have been redeemed.

Valerie M
President of a professional technologies consulting firm

Zinnia

Arms reached out to the sun goddess
Hands full of auburn, crimson and gold.
Abundant hues on fire;
That echoes the colors of life.
Warmed by sweet lemony rays of sun
And cooled by a soft breeze unseen,
I reach out that much further
With a palette to charm
The ice of wintry hearts
I beg mercy to remain
As innocent and beautiful
As I once began as seed.

Empathy

I weep when I gaze upon the chiseled pain on your face
A suffering that time cannot erase
I wait knowing life cannot delete the graffiti already written on your walls
Keenly aware that it is not stone that built these narrow halls
There is strength of softness that can not be washed away
That which makes the tower stand against its sway

I attempt to paint a different picture to hang inside this room

To cover up the years that have faded into gloom
But the hearth is much too small to hold the artist's weight
I leave the painted flowers outside your garden gate

There's a naked statue frozen in the garden of your youth
As the summer sun exposes what really is your truth
The winters have etched in stone the face we see today
But I still search to find the words to take your pain away.
As I stumble through the chatter I realize in a while
That I can't make you happy, I can only make you smile.

Juliet's Call
My lovely Juliet balcony
What irony to call it by name
As it beacons to me by night
To join her mortal plight

Her beautiful arched curves
That tower high above
A perfectly designed height
To take just one last flight

But I'll not visit her this eve
Her calls have not convinced
That we shall end this fight
As she beacons one more night.

Debra M
Hello my name is Debra M. I am just about 42 years old; I have been with my husband 19 years. I have one child from a previous relationship. I am a veteran of the United States military; serving one year on deployment oversees: Egypt for the Multi-Force Observers. I quit school at the age of 16 and did not receive my diploma until I turned 32. At that time or shortly thereafter, I enlisted in the National Guard. I began taking college classes after starting my tour of deployment oversees and have since received an associates of arts in criminal justice; and now, I am currently three classes away now from receiving my bachelor's degree in human services with a concentration on family and children. I am also a childhood survivor of sexual abuse; at the hands of multiple perpetrators within my family; and including one external family member. I spent most many years hiding my pain away or running from my trauma; it was not until I met my husband and gained self-confidence through my military training; where I began to heal and recover from the abuse. Now I advocate; write poetry, reach out and help as many survivors like me as I can.

From forevermore too nevermore… never, ever again….
It seemed as though the nightmares would never ascend; it seemed as if forever more; would never be again, as if off in some far away untouchable distant land. The fairy tale fantasy; that every child holds within the deepest inner most places; of their princess girls hearts and kingdom ruling, little boys minds; suddenly becomes a scary and very frightening place; where darkness and monsters are lurking but yet hidden from sight. They steal from the child's soul; attempting to take all that was once good. The trail of damage that is left behind; scars the inner spirit and wounds the child's mind., before too long it becomes too late, the destruction on the inside; has just become too great. The child breaks... No more fantasy land, fairytales no more, all that is left becomes desolate, isolated and they are left all alone; they'll need a hero; a brave warrior who'll lead them home: a true noble knight; to guide, to be a light, not afraid to fight; for them; with them, to help them get back home

Polly M
Polly M is a social justice advocate fighting to end child sexual abuse. She has just released her first book, *Cinder Blocks and Oven Racks*, which shares her story of sexual abuse as a child. She has volunteered with VOICE Today for the past four years, and in her role has spoken to many groups, appeared on numerous television and radio shows sharing her own story of sexual abuse and her passion to protect the next generation and led many survivor healing weekend retreats. She was awarded the prestigious 2015 Sapphire Award for her tireless dedication to the mission of VOICE Today. She fought diligently for legislative reform to extend the civil statute of limitations and House Bill 17 was signed into law on July 1, 2015. Her passion and commitment are never ending. Moore is the mother of one son and two granddaughters who she wants to provide a future of protection. Her greatest loves are her family, writing, the beach and gardening.

<u>Angela's Poem</u>
I believe that The Lord speaks;
I believe that The Lord cries;
I believe that The Lord loves;
I believe that The Lord gives;
I believe that The Lord takes away;
I believe that The Lord sees;
And I also believe that one day The Lord saw a need in the screams and cries that he heard on earth. I believe that He answered the tear filled prayers of millions by delivering a blessed soul, with a blessing caressed by a deeper love and an unknown strength to an unborn baby on earth.
I believe that The Lord appointed this blessed soul to a baby and while in the womb, He whispered to her a promise with this blessing that, she shall have courage and a strength that millions will have never seen. She will not only be one of the survivors, but she will return, time and time again to reveal His path and lead the way out of the blistering pain of child sexual abuse and show them how to heal.
I believe that The Lord only allows a few to have these precious gifts and blessings.
And I also believe that The Lord looked upon a woman as she slept and told her that she shall name her,
Angela.

Patricia
I'm 38 years old
I live in New York and I'm ready to tell my story!
Letter to a monster n my journey to healing!!

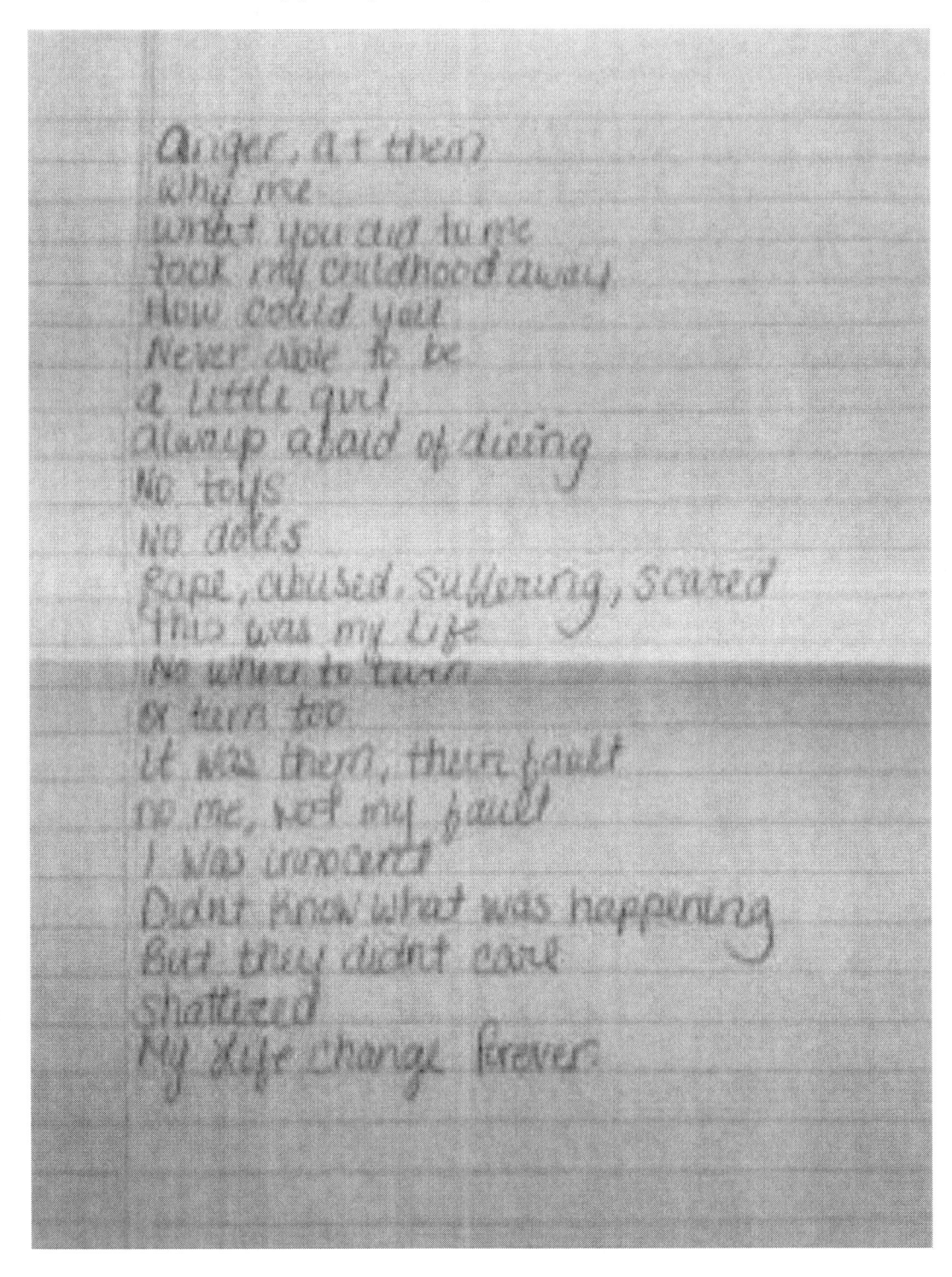

Anger, at them
Why me
What you did to me
Took my childhood away
How could you
Never able to be
a little girl
Always afraid of dieing
No toys
No dolls
Rape, abused, suffering, scared
This was my life
No where to turn
or turn too
It was them, their fault
no me, not my fault
I was innocent
Didn't know what was happening
But they didn't care
Shattered
My life change forever

I don't know what I would have been like if I haven't been abused. I don't know what kind of choices I would have made or how my life would have been different. I can't change any of that but I can change the course of my life now. Abuse set me on a path of self-destruction but my healing has set me on a new course of self love and self validation. I'M MAKING DECISIONS that are joy filled and life affirming. ABUSE DOSEN'T GET THE LAST WORD I DO

Letter To A Monster

I writing you this to finally get off my chest! How could u take away my childhood! Instead of being daddy's little girl u used me as a rag doll. How and why would u do this to me! U were supposed to be a father n protect me instead u used me and my mom done nothing to protect her own daughter from this monster. U get remarried and u allowed the same thing to continue.

I was afraid, scared to tell anybody but guess what I speak out after 30 years!!! This is my JOURNEY to HEALING!!!

My Journey

You think talking about abuse is hard, try living it!

I wrote a 10-page letter about my abuse. I was sexually abused by my real father AND from my mother's husband who I refuse to call a step-father. The abuse took place when I was a few months old from my real father. After my parent's got a divorce, the other abuse (from my mom's new husband) was taking place from ages 8-13. I remember every word and every move. I never told anyone cause I was told he would kill me.

Well, I finally opened up after 30 years and I have survived and lived to tell my story.
MY JOURNEY TO A NEW PERSON, MY HEALING!!!
What kept me going and helped me to not give up and to keep moving forward, was the strength I found when I had my children. Now, I have moved on and also found strength in my supportive boyfriend who helps to keep me going!
I keep my mind on positive things and the bad memories are stored away in my memory bank. I keep busy with my life and through this new found strength by sharing my story, I want to help and inspire others! By talking about my story, I'm not ashamed anymore; I moved on and am flying free!!!!

April R
April R is currently a meditation instructor, writer, and poet. She is also currently a member of RAINN's Speakers Bureau. Her area of interest is the intersection between meditation and creative writing, and their use together as tools in the awareness and management of PTSD and recovery from sexual trauma. She obtained her MAMS (Master of Applied Meditation Studies) from an Institute of Graduate Studies in Pennsylvania and is currently a meditation instructor there for the community. She has also instructed meditation at Pennsylvania State campus, for faculty and staff; and other facilities, for adults in the Philadelphia area with intellectual and developmental disabilities. She obtained her RN/BSN from the university in Florida and practiced in the fields of medical surgery, labor and delivery. She is also a veteran Captain of the United States Air Force where she served as both an active duty member and as a reservist. She currently lives in Pennsylvania where she is also a wife, mother, ballroom dancer, and proud survivor of childhood sexual abuse.

Early Reaping
A crow carried my soul away
Too many years before I passed
Beyond my body breaking low
I parted gladly in his grasp
Not soon enough for saving though
I was no longer fit for that
Having been born savagely so
Ravaged like hell before this act
He flew in through the window
His winging swirled the shattered glass
Swooping he scooped my spirit up
And gave me leave from living fast
But what to do with wispy me
Pitied much sooner than was tasked
We are each other's chore forever
More with purgatory ticking past

Triggered
I am marked
But I do not notice
Yet / The slightest pressure
Triggers an explosion
And a hollow-point projectile
Slices through my atmosphere
Slamming into me
Shredding upon entry
DAMN / I never ever see it coming
I am hit in my blind spot
So hard I swivel
My brain sloshing quick
In my fractured skull
I am disoriented
My vision narrows to tunnel
I am suddenly sweating
From every pore
Profusely frightened
Blood is pulled from my limbs

I am numb, shaking, and cooling
My resources pumping and pooling
My vital organs primed and filling for survival
And then, I am angry
WHAT THE FUCK!
I am so tired of this
Trigger-ignorant culture
And the concentric circles of my psyche
Always available for target practice
Until I am left riddled
And so full of holes
I cannot patch them fast enough
Before another FLASH
BANG
And I am thrown back
Again
To the moment when
I said no
But he did not listen

Wading Through
I will not censor part of me
Which begs to be expressed
Because it shatters the illusion
Reveals the human mess

There is no way around it
Only the wading through
Up to my neck in all of it
Is all I know to do

Perhaps I'll sit a moment
Stay with the stink and then
Investigate bacteria
'Till I am up to move again

I see all of you around me
Also trying to make sense
I can't look away or decorate
Or cover up the stench

I do not mind the stopping still
To have a look around
Be with the shit that bubbles up
The only way I've found

To engage my life and all of it
As it shows itself to me
I'll use it as fertilizer
Composting crap creatively

Maria S
Maria S. has a Master of Science degree in Environmental Health Management from a School of Public Health in Massachusetts and worked as an environmental health scientist for 22 years doing research and writing technical reports until chronic physical pain prevented her from continuing to work. A ruptured disc in her neck and subsequent neck surgery triggered her chronic myofascial neck pain. After two years of untenable pain, she discovered through specialized physical therapy that her physical pain was strongly linked to past trauma, including being molested when she was 10 years old. Once she discovered this connection, her pain became less severe, but it is still with her every day. Now she is taking a shot at poetry and creative writing to share her experience with others.

Remembering
I woke up frozen from a dream
It sparked a memory
Untouched and pristine

The perfect life
I'd believed to be true
Was just a crafty, cunning ruse

Silence was the only way
To carry on
Through another day

When days and years and decades amassed
My body could no longer hide
The painful truth of its past

My conscious mind buried it deep
To finally reveal it in my sleep

My mind was so clever
So it thought
To keep this event from my memory forever

Thirty-two years without a trace
I'd hidden it well
But at what price?

Now physical pain has stolen 10 years of my life
For a one-time act
That has caused me pure strife

The shame that came with what he did
Is so engrained
Inside my brain

I work and work to set it free

Yet the shame stands firm
Like an ancient tree

Fear and anger are close behind
Lurking in the shadows
Of my subconscious mind

How could such a small little act
Have such an indelible impact?

The terrified mind
Of a 10-year old girl
Cannot process what this means to her

Trust is gone
What is love?
Repress it all

Trauma
The assault was not violent
Though my mind might disagree
Upon recovering the memory
The nightmare consumed me

The panic and fear
From inside my soul
Has come alive
To take its toll

I fought it off for 32 years
I did a great job
Hiding those tears

For such a long time my life was just swell
I cruised along, that is, until
The memory came back
And I entered Hell

Anger, fear, and shame abound
A piercing, stabbing, stinging sound
They take my body to my knees
Begging for Mercy
Please, please, please!!

Re-living the shame and the panic and fear
Made me realize this trauma's undoubtedly real

A primal scream
Set off by deep breathing
Tells me there's something inside I've been shielding

I remembered what he did to me
He touched me inappropriately

The thoughts that festered decades long
Transformed themselves to a neck gone wrong

A ruptured disc was the first undeniable sign
That the fortress inside me was not at all fine

My mind could not face
The awful truth
Of what had happened to me
In my youth

So my body was to be the proof
Of an ill deep inside like a twisted old root

Suppressing emotions does not do the trick
The pain in still there
It's a wound hard to lick

The Voice Inside
The voice in my head says things I can't hear
The silent words are driving the car

The voice of Shame is at the helm
Passengers Fear, Anger, and Vulnerability are vying for space
In the front bench seat
Of the old wood-paneled station wagon
Of my youth

They recklessly careen around corners
Mocking the straight and easy path they prefer not to follow
I know they're there now
Yet they played me for a fool for 32 years
I danced along oblivious to their evil ways
Until they crashed into a brick wall while I slept

This subconscious voice is clearly heard
By my physical being
Traumatic memories are stored deep within
Muscles tense and stiffen in a knee-jerk reaction

The broken record plays and plays
Circling under the needle of my old banged up record player
A piercing sound that only a dog hears

The silent voices—as there are many—sit exposed
Deer in the headlights
Now I can hear them
And when I do, there's less tension, less physical pain
Though my psyche is heavily burdened instead
So they retreat back to their silent ways when they catch me off guard
They're weakened by my knowledge
But still persistent in their havoc-wreaking ways

The voices in my head must relinquish the wheel
Let me drive home, please
It's safer that way

Ashley S
Ashley S is a survivor of same-sex sexual assault and domestic violence. She has fought many battles in an attempt to educate others about her experience. When she was ready to tell her story she met with much opposition, whether it was a college professor telling her that her experience was "not statistically significant" or being consistently told that women cannot rape other women. Ashley is a fierce warrior for social justice and refuses to keep her story to herself. She received a Bachelor's Degree in Sociology in 2006 from a university in Georgia. Recently, she returned to the university to pursue an additional Bachelor's Degree in English with an emphasis on creative writing. Her eyes are set on a graduate program in Celtic Studies as well as a career as a writer. She hails from Georgia.

A Monument to the Moment
In the psychosis of the moment
I faced her down, gripped
by the pain of shame. Now,
in this mourning air, I construct a constant
reminder. Brick by painful brick I build
recalling my loss of rationale as
I laid silently still, waiting
for the moment to pass undetected.
I question this monument, my testament
to human suffering— surely my ache cannot be
the visceral result of violation so whole
that there was never any room for love. But
I build and try not to break
each time I realize that at any point
I could have screamed.

The Survivor Speaks
I was told today that I am
in remission; that you,
my human carcinogen,
have graciously relaxed your grip.
You are often far from my mind,
our experience seems to be a mere nightmare
the waking world cannot dream.
I am in remission though I can never forget.
I push my primal pain to the periphery
plodding small steps to recovery.
My slow success will one day be permanent
this widespread infection will not win
and all the words I have uttered for you
will be rendered speechless.

Adriana S

Adriana S is a 20 year old college junior residing in California, where she was born and raised as the daughter of Cuban-Italian immigrants. Following the incidents that occurred her freshman year, she has participated in and has spoken at various events for survivors of sexual assault and rape. After a brief hiatus, she has begun to write and perform spoken word poetry again, which has brought her healing. Pursuing a double major in Political Science and Spanish, she hopes to affect public policy surrounding sexual assault on campus, a subject that she has researched in many of her politics courses.

<u>A Letter to My Rapist</u>
It has been a whole year,
And still, I cannot find the words to, I can't find the thoughts to
It's been months since I've talked to you,
But every time we see each other, we can't deny that something's there
And I'm not talking about romance.
Something stops us in our tracks if we accidentally make eye contact.
My heart does not flutter, my insides start to shudder when I think I see your face in a crowd.
I weave every which way, taking the road less-traveled to avoid the paths you make.
Crafted carefully, this cautious calligraphy courses through all parts of my day as I envision
What I would do if I ever saw you inching towards me again.
I can't believe it's been a year,
Because I still flinch whenever I hear your name,
And I'm ready to run when I see your face.
I hate how you still have the power to ruin my day by not even doing anything.
At night I can't sleep,
Tossing and turning, My body keeps yearning for rest that will never come.
For with sleep come nightmares that always end with me screaming
Thrashing, gnawing, clawing
At anything I can get my hands on, doing everything I was too scared to do those nights.
In my dreams, they brand me a liar
Using my words against me, twisting them to make me the bad guy.
I can't believe it's been a year
Because guilt washes over me in tidal waves.
I'm still trying to piece together what happened, but each time I do
Memories flood my mind until I'm shaking
Struggling to push you from my conscience.
I'm overwhelmed with the thought that no one believes me,
That I have to relive it every time someone asks me to defend myself.
And maybe it's been a year,
But I can't shake the paranoid sense that someone's watching me.
Can't shake the impulse to fight
At night when it's dark out is when I remember you most.
So it's no wonder I try to avoid the 12am abyss, stumbling past dimly-lit street corners
Sounds of laughing and drunken revelry
But all I see are semblances of the nights you hurt me.
Shadows of a struggle I couldn't possibly have won.
So when I see you those nights
Don't be surprised as I turn the other way.
Because even after a year,
I still can't stomach a glimpse of you.

Marilyn T
Marylyn Louisa T, born and raised in California, completed an MA in Counseling Psychology Community Mental specializing in addictions in 2012 and volunteered for ten years as a substance abuse counselor and intern therapist at a free clinic. I chose that clinic because of the writing on the door: HEALTH CARE IS A RIGHT NOT A PRIVILEGE. I believed that when I first read it in 1967, and I still believe it today, although the clinic has now been absorbed by a corporate entity that removed not only the writing, but the *entire* door. This motivated me to use my own skills and education to develop Healing Through Writing Workshops for female survivors of sexual abuse, relationship violence and neglect. Workshops include some guided meditation, community drumming, creative artwork, and chakra awareness exercises. I also developed a trauma workshop to help parents with addicted children work through the fear, anxiety and collateral damage of addiction. I have been an avid quilt maker for more than 30 years, and hope someday to incorporate the fine art of quilting into a therapeutic storytelling modality. I have one daughter, who is always my heart and inspiration.

Soul Survivor
San Francisco summer 1969…corner of Haight and Ashbury – we are
Making Love Not War, surrounded by the scent of patchouli-pot, and smoky sandalwood,
Grateful Dead and Whiskey-Janis rasping out a Southern Comfort hymn.
That's where I spied him, strolling through the Haight, aiming just for me, linen drawstrings swinging and bare feet slapping on concrete cracks. Sleepy eyes, hair like
    Jesus bushy, bearded, wild golden-sun.
    I had seen this one before…Mr. Ardourel's 7th period Creative Writing Class; he was a senior member, detached, delicious, a hippie in the works,
        never even glanced in my direction…
Until today. Today he grabbed my eyes and crowned me with a wispy daisy chain.
Christened himself Dennis, with a panhandle address and a party invitation. / Starts at 9.
I was right on time, in my gauzy peasant top and frayed denim mini, Cuban-heeled kicks filched from grandma's closet and a sling-bag draped across my chest.
        I tap on beveled glass and Dennis opens up. He offers me a Ripple swig and leads me   through some shuddering French Doors.
We rock to Hendrix, sway to Cream, swig and laugh and kiss like polar magnets.
Up close, I notice he is pock-marked, craggy, sour-mouthed and heavy. Heavy on me.
I shift my weight a little, edgy giggle,
try to turn my face away. Rough hands twisted in my hair. / Oh, NO! NO, YOU DON'T! Not tonight!!
The slap is a terrifying surprise. Cap snaps loose on a back tooth. Scalp is screaming from the roots. Forearm choking off my air….Southern Comfort…please don't hurt me, Grateful
Dead…please don't kill me.
    "Shut the fuck up." Another slap…struggling, calculating, blood drops sticky on my lip and cheek. I kick out and fly toward the safety of those French Doors. The knob won't turn…doors won't budge…craggy-heavy-pock-marked fury slams me to the wall and I know what I must do.
I surrender. Go limp. Let the top rip, the skirt lift. Stay quiet…move only with the monster.
Pushing…Cursing…grunting turns to snoring…rolls off me in a wasted bunch.
I am up like a shot, tangled in denim and gauze, heart bursting,
    Cuban heels smashing through the fancy glass. I am out, gone…
    Racing through the Haight, past hookah bars and Head Shops, black light poster blinks in the window of Bound Together Books…
    All you need is love
    Love is all you need…
    And the courage to restore your own
        Unsinkable / Soul.

Sylvia T

SHATTERED INNOCENCE RENEWED

Just a young girl in mind and body, attached and detached at the same time. Happy, secure, promoted to one family, and demoted from another. I was introduced to God and understood from where blessings flowed. Surrounded by love for it was my emotional nourishment ever since I remember. And I was never famished. At peace with the manner of things mostly, until my not a stranger did something strange. He took my girly girls order of things and left me broken and shocked, and imprisoned in my young girly girl's being. Shattered? Oh yes! Cursed for something I did not cause! Why take my girly hood and force me into my womanhood before time? Why make a liar out of me? Make me cry hidden tears, forcing me to keep secrets in an uneasy way... Why? Why? Why took over my girly girls presence? It created in me a spirit of fear. Hey! Where was my security? Security! It did not answer when my soul summoned it. So, I became unanchored. Yet I had to pretend that my girly hood still existed. I wanted it not to change but there was nothing left of her. But then, I remembered my lifeline called, LOVE! The love taught to me was genuine and unique. Even in the midst of my bewilderment, and grief I remembered love. My girly girl was not the same. Oh how I cherished her. I did not want to let her go before I was ready. I did not put her away. She was stripped away and with her went the solemnest and innocence of a child's play, laughter, pretends, and make believe. It all vanished quickly! It was a dark shadow in my life so I asked God not to let it be my life. Please Sir, dress me in the gifts of your will. Dressed me with peace, forgiveness, and acceptance. Comfort the memories of my girly girl woes. Let your light shine in me for her. For the land of peace and purpose is where I will dwell my girly girl self and I will always treasure lessons of renewed strength and self love!

Wil T

Shadows Of My Former Self
When I was just a boy
I was
Quiet
Shy
Abused
Used
Unseen
Unheard

As a result I became internally adept to express myself through the thoughts in my head and hauntings of spoken and unspoken words.

The content there in I kept tucked away on a private shelf. My mind used, my body abused and spirit discarded, I silently cried for help.

None could save me until the day would come I was ready to share the expression of the beautiful person i have become today as I say good bye to the shadows of my former self.

Diva T
Actress (Stage, Television, and Film), Awarded the 2015 Best Black Female, "Rising Star" in the Arts by The National Black Women in Jazz and Arts Association, Private Coaching for beginners, Inspirational/Transformational Personal Growth Life Coach, Activist, Spoken Word Artist, Published Author, Community Ambassador Spokesperson for Fulton County Based Organization "YouthSpark" Founder of "Not On My Watch Endeavors" (NOMWE) An Anti-Trafficking/ Anti-Slavery Movement

THE RE-CREATION OF MYSELF
Like the ugly outer appearance of a bad story told over and over again
I kept retelling, Therefore, reliving the pain of a life so badly misunderstood
I was searching for someone to understand, but no one could, as if they should
I mean, the whole time it was all about me, There was no one else to blame, I was just running from the truth and shame, of what I'd allowed myself to believe about me, and then became. But you see it was a process that I had to go through, before I could change.

The many lives that I have lived, the many masks that I have worn
Were all predetermined before the day that I was born
I remember being touched in a place, that was not of good taste
for a girl of my age, transforming my innocence into a bitter sweet rage
The mathematics of my mind began calculating the reality of it all
hearing inner voices, crying, whispering, screaming, begging "Don't give up, Hang on, Stand tall"

So I devised a way to survive, to stay alive, until the day that I would arrive
I became determined to deal with the lustful and unsolicited dreaded touches
and the eye-opening awareness of all of the insincere and contrived "I Love You Muches"
I became heaven bent focused on making it through, because my time to reign over my life again, was much too far overdue
But on the day I was to arrive, I suddenly realized, that I had to first learn to survive all of the deceptions, lies, cries and false alibis, being hurled at me, all at one time

My God, for awhile, I thought I was going to lose my mind, But knowledge of truth is much more sublime.
Flashbacks of hearing my mother say, "I wouldn't take a million dollars for you, But for another one just like you, I wouldn't pay a dime!

So, I guess helping to instill self-esteem, wasn't an issue in those days
But in order to have some, I had to create other ways, I began going through the process phase by phase, and no, it's not always been easy, and sometimes I still do fail, slippin, dippin and dabbling into things they said would surely send me to hell
But so much for that my dear, because I am still here, and as long as I am still here, I can still change, and rearrange, how I really want my life to be
So thus began the journey of "The Re-Creation of Me"

First, I stopped all but the most undeniably gotta have sins, and then I dropped all of the lying, crying, begging and fake friends
I then removed myself from an environment, whose world had become my beast
I humbled myself, admitted I didn't know it all, and began to pray, as I initiated my journey, towards the east

Now this journey is not an easy one, and no one said it would be

But it will help to make my life more purposeful, removing the veils from my minds' eyes so that I can more clearly see
I have learned that, It is love, understanding and prayer, that is the catalyst in the creation of change
And as in the metamorphosis of change, emerges the beautiful butterfly
From the dark, ugly, outer appearance of the cocoon, in which she hides in shame.
But divine intervention, removes her from this dark existence
With beauty intact, No indications of any ugliness or shame left.
Just the good work, God has done, and is still doing in me, in the re-creation of myself

Yes this is my story , this is true and of that I cannot lie, nor will I deny
That world was my dark cocoon, Oh, but I am now that beautiful, beautiful

BUTTERFLYYYY!!!

<u>THE ABDUCTION OF MY CHILDHOOD</u>
Fragmented pictures of hide and go seek
Stalked by shadows that made me afraid and weak
Bedtime stories half told in my head
The horrible touches that made me wish I were dead

No one believed me, so I kept it inside
Crawled away in my mind with no one to confide
The prodding and pawing I had to endure
To become invisible was my only cure

Who had time to play hopscotch! I was fighting for my life
A thousand times in my mind I killed him with my hate knife
No child on this earth deserves to undergo such betraying treatment
It disavows their mind, and sends their hearts into bereavement
And what penalty should be imposed on one of such arrogance and huff
Well I think to burn in hell isn't quite good enough

Because you see there is just no way to determine the damage that's been done
To the little one, whose childhood should have been fun
Now I know they all say that there comes a time when we must forgive and put the past behind us
And to live a healthy, positive and productive life, I know that I must

But how do I process, all that's happened to me?
To live life without remembering, I cannot see
And that's only part of what his sickness has done to me
But to forget, for just one night, my God I wish I could
Mommy, may I have back my childhood?

<u>A WAY WHILE BACK</u>
A way while back, my innocence was exploited and abused.
Emotionally and Spiritually broken, I became so lost and confused
I felt I must have deserved it, I was a child, what did I know
And the bitterness from self-loathing began to grow more and more.

A way while back, when my life was way off track, I was drawn to self-abuse along with all the negative people I used to attract; And the order of the day was to smoke weed or smoke crack, and blurred by the fact, that I didn't have the will or the knowledge on how to fight back, like a lion seeking to devour me my soul was attacked and all my world became blacker than black

A way while back, my life was so shattered and cracked, And I could no longer maintain the urge or desire to retract; So out of pure desperation, I attempted to contact...The Deeper Side Of Me
So I closed my eyes and fell to my knees and began to pray,
...., Dear Lord, Save me from myself, save me from the self destruction that I have brought my way. Help me to learn the importance of who you have made me to be, And Lord, most of all, help me to recognize the God in me

I pray you help me to develop an unprecedented trust in you, I pray for your wisdom and guidance in everything that you do

Your magnificent grace is so unfathomable, that I hardly understood,
How you could love me even when I had been so bad, you could still be so good
It was that revelation that led me back to you so willingly, No one had to make me or force, Oh no, it's where I wanted to be

A way while back, back there, back then , is a place I never want to be a part of again. You see, I was spiritually blind, living in sin, way back then
Now I know, I can't go back and change things from what happened before   But, one thing I do know for certainty and for sure

When I began to pray to God to save me from the life that I was living, I believed in his words and trusted in him, when he whispered in my heart and soul and said, My Beloved Child....YOU ARE NOW FORGIVEN!!

Mercedes W
Mercedes W is a spiritual intuitive, teacher, artist and author. She has written two healing systems which were the post traumatic spiritual growth after experiencing a home invasion: The Soul Inspired Tune Up® and Visionscapes®. Her art began to emerge through her in 2012 when she unexpectedly painted a piece at an afternoon workshop that she thought was quite good. My work comes through Spirit. In Spirit and through Spirit each painting, meditation, story or poem has emerged. Her work is primarily dedicated to bringing out the inner voices and dreams then turning those dreams into the passionate Visionscapes we live. "I am very excited about the conversations that are coming forth, the voices that are breaking their silence and the courage of women telling their stories."

Today I Celebrate™... Sacred Deserving!
"I deserve"
I let each word warm over me like a ray of sunshine
Bask!
Sacred are the personal rites of deserving.
Bask!
Sacred are the personal rites of pleasing Self.
Bask!
Sacred are the personal rites of loving Self.
Bask!
Sacred are the rites of the Inner I Am
I deserve.
I deserve.
I deserve.
I Am Success. Success is My Sacred Right!

Today I Celebrate...Sacred Deserving!
Wants and desires are Divine Source's way of showing Its magnificent glory. When you accomplish something that is truly heartfelt and personal you beam light and love into the world. When you have come through the fire of transformation your survival is experiencing the Divine.

Your personal experience with accomplishment, living and success is vibrational certainty. For as we may have faith and belief there is no better testimony to the existence of Source than the full sensory experience of achievement. Bask in the wanting of your desires large and small. Bask in the moment-to-moment receiving. Bask in anticipation.

Treat your desires with sanctity. Create a ceremony around each that is personal and meaningful and with deliberate certainty bask in your rites of sacred deserving.

Today I Celebrate™... Courage!
Thrown into the fire pit.
Connecting with the Knowing.
Emerging transformed.
BEing as a sacred point of Light.
Walking back into the fire pit
To guide
To direct and
To love.
I Am Success. Success is My Sacred Right!

Today I Celebrate™... Courage!
To live a lesson does not always mean that you have to teach the lesson to someone else. If you feel the inner urging to do so know that you are courageous because to teach we have to have revisit and repurpose this darkness on your journey's path.

To see your survival blossom through the fear and pain of someone else is the reward here. It takes guts in the natural dimension and conviction in the spiritual.

Remember, their path is their path.
You are the tour guide.
Your firm hand in the gentle sway of their back is hope.
Divine Source is the conductor.

There are new lessons for you here as your unique gifts arise and take flight.

Out of the ashes....

Today I Celebrate™... The Discomfort Zone!
Going into new places where people
may not "accept" me.
Taking new risks that leads
to unknown territory.
Forging new relationships where I must trust
because there is no other option.
Today I stand in my discomfort. This is
My courage
My growth and
My expansion is here.
I Am Success! Success is My Sacred Right.

Today I Celebrate™... The Discomfort Zone!
Are you thinking, "Whoa! How did I get here?" Welcome to The Discomfort Zone, the place where you always dreamed of being.

Welcome. Seekers of their truth are welcome here. A way was made or how else would you be here. Time to plant your feet and feel the roots deep in the center of Earth Mother and look to the heavens (within or without) and seek the Divine Mother because now is the time to channel the mud of origin with the essence of manifestation and bring your dream to humanity.

Welcome! Behold! Realize!

Rachael W
My name is Rachael W, a 22-year-old transgender individual living in Florida. I utilize the pronoun set [they/them/theirs]. I am an advanced graduate student in mental health counseling specializing in trauma-focused care at a university in Florida. I hope to one day provide compassionate, informed counseling services to transgender survivors of rape and assault. I am a speaker of RAINN, a victim advocate, and a victim services volunteer. I am a passionate advocate for transgender rights and the rights of sexual assault survivors. Currently, I am in my third semester of my graduate degree. I enjoy making jewelry, stuffed animals, cats, 90s music, pizza, reading existential literature, and playing survival horror video games. My favorite superhero is Batwoman and my favorite villain is Venom. I sponsor a cat named Fred at Blind Cat Rescue whom I adore. I spend most of my time voraciously consuming my textbooks for class. When I'm not in class, sleeping, or in a textbook you can find me in a little town in Florida, spending time with my wonderful partner, a 2-L law student. My poetry tends to be dark, but my demeanor is lively. I love to help others, smile, and have fun.

loose items
when leaving someone i make no mess
i sweep the floor of any remnants of me
statistically, this will cut down on the sick grins as they relive their glory days
as someone who could paint orchid purple and coffee brown bruises on virgin skin
i drink down the embraces that turned to slaps in a cracked mug with no origin
i don't leave my CDs for you to replay your thrills again
you're not allowed to have memories of me
because i'm dusting them off your shelf and vacuuming them from your ugly beige carpet

retch
love,
confused with power and control,
tastes dirty on my tongue

disrespect
you crossed my boundaries
you aligned yourself with all of my causes
but you were there for the wrong reasons
you are not entitled to my body
nor my story
nor my safe space
it's not for you, and never will be
what you are is a robber
you slink behind compassionate people
turning them
against me
they will believe you of course
because i didn't win the race of deceiving looks
you have them all going for you
keep using them
you'll end out on top
but you won't
because a survivor
a true survivor
can grasp your heart
open it

and see,
honey,
you're full of shit.

<u>organ donor</u>
when i turned sixteen my license didn't have the mark of an organ donor
back then, i saw my organs as one of the few things left as everything was getting worse
they kept me warm at night
i was selfish
during the five years i had to think about it, i wanted to give them away so bad
the path to my uterus had been marred by you, and my brain stewed in your callous remarks
i would do anything to change my status
i was selfish
when i turned twenty-one my license proudly displayed the mark
my organs mean something now
my heart can give love as fierce as a dam bursting, and my lungs breathe in pure air
no longer selfish
when i move on
and all i can offer that is that which is tangible
i hope that you- whoever you are
will take my organs, paint the night with them, kiss the trees, and love just like me

Tania W
My name is Tania W, and I am a divorced, single mother of 2 adopted teenage girls, and I am also a middle school teacher. I survived date rape at the age of 16 that resulted in a pregnancy. My mother forced me to abort the child, something I have never recovered from, and I hope my poem will help someone out there. If I could do anything in my life over again, I would have found a way to not have that abortion.

Haiku
I begged you to stop
You had your way with me still
Now I'm lost and alone

Lost, But Not Gone Forever
You said you loved me
That you would always be there for me
Yet you had your way with me
Violated me
Raped me
Then walked away from me
Did you know you left me with your seed?
Did you know you changed my life forever?
Or were you just thinking about yourself
Your own selfish needs and satisfaction?
Why did I mean so little to you?
That you could use and abuse me
And never think of how it would hurt me
My baby, our baby, never had a chance
Because of your selfishness I was on my own
Now my only chance to see my child
Will be when I'm dead and gone
Only then will I be able to hold my child
Your child
Our child
The one you so callously disregarded
After you threw me away
Like yesterday's trash.

Untitled Living
Strong-minded with beauty and brains
Coming together as one
Willing to change
Stop smoking weed to cope with your pain
We are worth more than we think
Society always looking and judging
It's time for a change
Through the cries and the pain
Damn nothing stays the same
Young, gifted, and Black—It's not a dream
Our future is coming
It's not what it seems
Dream big
It will turn into reality
MY future, MY voice
This is where it's at
Yesterday I found my voice
Today I'm here to shout about it!
~Voices

Amiya

Yummy Pearl
I once was a slave
I once was tight
I smoked a blunt
And things didn't go right.

I was on the street
Selling my soul for meat
With nothing to spare
And nothing to eat

I thought I loved him
I thought he was the one
Until he stole it from me
And my body went numb.
I obeyed his commands
He was my god.
Something told me to change
So I had to drop the rod

I still am weak until this day
But I know soon, God will take the pain away
I pray every day for change to come
And now I am changed
The damage is done

Valendia

FREE STYLE
I'm black
I'm proud
I'm THICK
I'm loud
I'm beautiful
I'm nice
Add some flavor
Some spice
But seriously
I love myself
I'm feeling this rhyme
Didn't take much time

National Resources

What is sexual violence?
Sexual violence is any sexual act or attempted sexual act by violence or coercion, unwanted sexual comments or advances, or any acts to traffic another person, regardless of the relationship between the victim and offender.

What are the forms of sexual violence?
- Rape or Sexual Assault
- Sexual Harassment
- Incest
- Unwanted sexual contact or touching
- Sexual exploitation
- Exhibitionism or Voyeurism
- Intimate Partner Sexual Violence
- Child sexual assault or incest

Who can be a victim of sexual violence?
Anyone can be a victim of sexual violence. Women or men, girls or boys, adults or children can all be victims of sexual violence.

Where can I learn more about sexual violence?
To learn more about all forms of sexual violence and where to get help visit:
www.rainn.org

To find out more information about staying safe, legal protection or your state laws visit:
www.womenslaw.org

If you are a male survivor or sexual violence, and want more information on healing and recovery visit:
www.malesurvivor.org

If you or someone you know is a victim of sexual violence or may need help, call:
National Sexual Assault Hotline: 1-800-656-HOPE (4673)

Additional Resources
Suicide Prevention Lifeline: 1-800-273-TALK (8255)
National Domestic Violence Hotline: 1-800-799-7233
National Human Trafficking Hotline: 1-888-373-7888
National Center for Missing and Exploited Children: 1-800-THE-LOST (1-800-843-5678)

Resource Bibliography

Books about Sexual Violence

Against Our Will: Men, Women, and Rape. 1993. Susan Brownmiller

Asking for It: The Alarming Rise of Rape Culture--and What We Can Do about It. 2015. Kate Harding

The Beginning and End of Rape: Confronting Sexual Violence in Native America. 2015. Sarah Deer

A Call to Action: Women, Religion, Violence, and Power. 2014. Jimmy Carter

The Comfort Women: Sexual Violence and Postcolonial Memory in Korea and Japan. 2009. C. Sarah

Conquest: Sexual Violence and American Indian Genocide. 2015. by Andrea Smith

The Crisis of Campus Sexual Violence: Critical Perspectives on Prevention and Response. 2015. Sara Carrigan Wooten and Roland W. Mitchell

Dear Sister: Letters from Survivors of Sexual Violence. 2014. by Lisa Factora-Borchers and Aishah Shahidah Simmons.

Desert Flower. 2009. Waris Dirie and Cathleen Miller

Expressive Therapies for Sexual Issues: A Social Work Perspective. 2012. Sana Loue

Finding Fish: A Memoir. 2001. Antwone Q. Fisher and Mim E. Rivas

Gender in Refugee Law: From the Margins to the Centre. 2014. Efrat Arbel and Catherine Dauvergne

Girls Like Us: Fighting for a World Where Girls Are Not for Sale, an Activist Finds Her Calling and Heals Herself. Rachel Lloyd

In an Abusive State: How Neoliberalism Appropriated the Feminist Movement against Sexual Violence. 2008. Kristin Bumiller

Infidel. 2007. Ayaan Hirsi Ali

Introduction to Global Health. 2013. Kathryn H. Jacobsen

Johan Galtung: Pioneer of Peace Research. 2013. Johan Galtung

The Power of the Powerless: Women's Work, Sexual Violence and Autonomy in Ciudad Juarez (1994-2004). 2014. Ana M. Bergareche

Preventing Sexual Violence: Interdisciplinary Approaches to Overcoming a Rape Culture. 2014. Nicola Henry and Anastasia Powell

Rape, Incest, Battery: Women Writing Out the Pain. 2000. Miriam Harris

Reclaiming Our Voices: An Anthology Honoring Domestic Violence and Sexual Assault. 2015. Carla Christopher-Waid and T.L. Christopher-Waid

Redefining Rape. 2013. Estelle B. Freedman

Saving Safa: Rescuing a Little Girl from FGM. 2015. Waris Dirie

Sexual Assault and Abuse (Confronting Violence Against Women). 2015. Ann Byers

Sexual Violence and Armed Conflict. 2011. Janie L. Leatherman

Sexual Violence: The Sin Revisited. 2005. Marie M. Fortune

Sexual Violence: The Unmentionable Sin. 1983. Marie M. Fortune

Sexual Violence during War and Peace: Gender, Power, and Post-Conflict Justice in Peru (Studies of the Americas). 2014. Jelke Boesten

Sexual Violence against Jewish Women during the Holocaust (HBI Series on Jewish Women). 2010. Sonja M. Hedgepeth and Rochelle G. Saidel

Sexual Violence and Abuse [2 volumes]: An Encyclopedia of Prevention, Impacts, and Recovery. 2012. Judy L. Postmus

SLUT: A Play and Guidebook for Combating Sexism and Sexual Violence. 2015. Katie Cappiello and Meg McInerney

Sticks and Stones...and Words That Hurt Me: A Collection of Poetry and Short Stories In Support of Domestic Violence. 2014. Aurelia Maria Casey

Stolen Lullabies and Secret Impasses: Child Abuse, Sexual Assault & Domestic Violence Awareness Campaign 2015. Donna L. Quesinberry

Surviving Sexual Violence: A Guide to Recovery and Empowerment. 2011. Thema Bryant-Davis

Theorizing Sexual Violence (Routledge Research in Gender and Society). 2011. Renée J. Heberle and Victoria Grace

Terror in the Heart of Freedom: Citizenship, Sexual Violence, and the Meaning of Race in the Postemancipation. 2009. Hannah Rosen

Violence against Women: Current Theory and Practice in Domestic Abuse, Sexual Violence and Exploitation. 2013. Nancy Lombard

The Violence of Care: Rape Victims, Forensic Nurses, and Sexual Assault Intervention. 2014. Sameena Mulla

Understanding Sexual Violence: A Study of Convicted Rapists (Perspectives on Gender). 1990. Diana Scully

Voices of Survivors: Silent No More...Survivors Speak Out. 2009. Vanilla Heart Publishing

Wartime Rape and Sexual Violence: An examination of the perpetrators, motivations, and functions of sexual violence. 2013. Alana Fangrad

White Women, Rape, and the Power of Race in Virginia, 1900-1960. 2004. Lisa Lindquist Dorr

Who Will Cry for the Little Boy? 2010. Antwone Q. Fisher

Woman-to-Woman Sexual Violence: Does She Call It Rape? (Northeastern Series on Gender, Crime, and Law). 2002. Lori B. Girshick

Dissertations about Sexual Violence

Attracting college men to sexual violence prevention: A multiple case study of male peer educators Deeds, Janice M.. The University of Nebraska - Lincoln, ProQuest Dissertations Publishing, 2009.

Being delivered: Spirituality in survivors of sexual violence. Knapik, Gregory Peter. Kent State University, ProQuest Dissertations Publishing, 2006.

Beyond raptus: Pedagogies and fantasies of sexual violence in late-medieval England Edwards, Suzanne M.. The University of Chicago, ProQuest Dissertations Publishing, 2006.

Communal riots, sexual violence and Hindu nationalism in post-independence Gujarat (1969-2002) Kumar, M. University of Oxford (United Kingdom), ProQuest Dissertations Publishing, 2010.

Dating violence and sexual assault among college men: Co-occurrence, predictors, and differentiating factors. Warkentin, Jennifer B.. Ohio University, ProQuest Dissertations Publishing, 2008.

Deconstructing sexual violence through the co-construction and telling of Mexican American gender histories. Carrillo, Iris Ylenia. University of Illinois at Urbana-Champaign, ProQuest Dissertations Publishing, 2010.

Developing Leaders of Character and Preventing Sexual Violence in the U.S. Military: Towards a Model of Respectful Sexuality. Arbeit, Miriam R.. Tufts University, ProQuest Dissertations Publishing, 2015.

An ethnography of sexual health and violence among township youth in South Africa Wood, K M. London School of Economics and Political Science (United Kingdom), ProQuest Dissertations Publishing, 2003.

Explaining sexual violence during civil war. Cohen, Dara Kay. Stanford University, ProQuest Dissertations Publishing, 2010.

An Exploratory Analysis of Sexual Violence and Rape Myth Acceptance at a Small Liberal Arts University. Wiscombe, Karla. University of Kansas, ProQuest Dissertations Publishing, 2012.

An exploratory study of teen dating violence in sexual minority youth. Reuter, Tyson R..University of Houston, ProQuest Dissertations Publishing, 2015.

Exploring risk factors among female undergraduate college students reporting the experience of sexual violence: A comparative analysis of African Americans and Caucasians. Memiah, Peter Njoroge. Morgan State University, ProQuest Dissertations Publishing, 2006.

Exposure to Dating/Sexual Violence and Health Risk Behaviors among Black, Hispanic, and White Female Adolescents. Lassiter, Teri Elizabeth. University of Medicine and Dentistry of New Jersey, ProQuest Dissertations Publishing, 2012.

Exposure to filmed sexual violence and attitudes toward rape. Weisz, Monica Grace. Universite de Montreal (Canada), ProQuest Dissertations Publishing, 1992.

Family related attitudes and beliefs influencing risk and support seeking among female victims of domestic and sexual violence in El Paso, Texas. Huerta, Diane Ilene. The University of Texas at El Paso, ProQuest Dissertations Publishing, 2014.

Gender inequality, normative violence, social disorganization and sexual violence against women: A cross-national investigation. Gubin, Alexandra. University of Massachusetts Amherst, ProQuest Dissertations Publishing, 2004.

HIV-risk behaviors and intimate partner violence in urban, adolescent girls: Impact of sexual relationship power and partner age differential. Volpe, Ellen M.. University of Rochester School of Nursing, ProQuest Dissertations Publishing, 2010.

The Impact of Race and Ethnicity on Sexual Violence: A Case Study on Underserved Populations in Minnesota. Bolstad, Lindsay. Minnesota State University, Mankato, ProQuest Dissertations Publishing, 2014.

Interpersonal violence and HIV sexual risk behaviors: The influence of alcohol harm reduction and early initiation of sex work among female sex workers in Mombasa, Kenya. Parcesepe, Angela M.. The University of North Carolina at Chapel Hill, ProQuest Dissertations Publishing, 2015.

Intimate partner violence and HIV sexual risk in Latino gay men: The role of sexual self-efficacy and participation in difficult sexual situations. Feldman, Matthew Brian. Columbia University, ProQuest Dissertations Publishing, 2005.

Intimate partner violence and sexual harassment in women veterans: Prevalence, provider inquiry, and associated mental health outcomes. Rose, Isabel Merchant. State University of New York at Albany, ProQuest Dissertations Publishing, 2001.

Lean on me: informal social networks and the prevention of intimate partner violence in sexual minority communities. Lippy, Caroline. Georgia State University, ProQuest Dissertations Publishing, 2011.

Linguistic strategies in the representation of sexual violence: Norwegian narrative perspectives Palsson, S. The University of Edinburgh (United Kingdom), ProQuest Dissertations Publishing, 2006.

Male sexual violence victimization: Definitions, epidemiological profile, and psychological impact Choudhary, Ekta. West Virginia University, ProQuest Dissertations Publishing, 2009.

News accounts of sexual violence against women and girls in the British daily national press Carter, C L. The University of Wales College of Cardiff (United Kingdom), ProQuest Dissertations Publishing, 1998.

Perpetrators of sexual violence within intimate relationships: Sexual offenders or male batterers? Picheca, Janice Elizabeth. University of Toronto (Canada), ProQuest Dissertations Publishing, 2006.

Philomela and her sisters: explorations of sexual violence in plays by British contemporary women dramatists (BL). Park, K R. University of Warwick (United Kingdom), ProQuest Dissertations Publishing, 1998.

Policy of abuse: A framework of public policy dimensions analyzing systematic sexual violence in Bosnia. Chary, Meena. Florida Atlantic University, ProQuest Dissertations Publishing, 2007.

Predictors of intimate partner violence in women's sexual minority relationships Gumienny, Leslie A.. Virginia Consortium for Professional Psychology (Old Dominion University), ProQuest Dissertations Publishing, 2010.

A preliminary examination of factors related to the comprehensiveness of sexual violence prevention efforts at Indiana institutions of higher education. Stolley, Lindsey Anne Vacek. Purdue University, ProQuest Dissertations Publishing, 2014.

The primary prevention of sexual violence against adolescents in Racine County and the Community Readiness Model. DeWalt, Theresa A.. Marquette University, ProQuest Dissertations Publishing, 2009.

Punctuated Silence: The International Response to Wartime Sexual Violence. Crawford, Kerry F.. The George Washington University, ProQuest Dissertations Publishing, 2014.

Reliability and Consistency of Risk Formulations in Assessments of Sexual Violence Risk Wilson, Catherine M.. Simon Fraser University (Canada), ProQuest Dissertations Publishing, 2013.

Religion and sexual violence in late Greco-Roman antiquity. Caldwell, John Matthew. Syracuse University, ProQuest Dissertations Publishing, 2003.

Rethinking War/Rape: Feminism, critical explanation and the study of wartime sexual violence, with special reference to the Eastern Democratic Republic of Congo. Kirby, Paul. London School of Economics and Political Science (United Kingdom), ProQuest Dissertations Publishing, 2012.

Revictimization in women's lives: An empirical and theoretical account of the links between child sexual abuse and repeated sexual violence. Haskell, Lori. University of Toronto (Canada), ProQuest Dissertations Publishing, 1999.

The role of violence in the social construction of intimate and sexual relationships, sexual risk taking, and parenting among low-income, inner city African Americans. Hatcherson, Jean. University of Connecticut, ProQuest Dissertations Publishing, 2009.

Rural women's experiences of sexual communication and sexual violence in marital and cohabitating heterosexual relationships. McCarthy, Patricia Frances. The Ohio State University, ProQuest Dissertations Publishing, 1995.

Sexual violence and correlates among women in HIV discordant union, Uganda. Emusu, Donath. The University of Alabama at Birmingham, ProQuest Dissertations Publishing, 2007.

Sexual violence and HIV risk behaviors in a nationally representative sample of American adult women. Stockman, Jamila K.. The Johns Hopkins University, ProQuest Dissertations Publishing, 2008.

Sexual violence as an image for divine retribution in the prophetic writings. Weems, Renita Jean. Princeton Theological Seminary, ProQuest Dissertations Publishing, 1989.

Sexual violence on campus: The relationship between sorority membership, fraternity contact, and alcohol consumption. Jordan-Simmons, Kym Michelle. University of Pittsburgh, ProQuest Dissertations Publishing, 2001.

Sexual violence prevention on college campus as a Clery Act requirement: Perceptions from the field. Gottlieb, Irina. University of Southern California, ProQuest Dissertations Publishing, 2008.

State-perpetrated wartime sexual violence in Latin America. Leiby, Michele. The University of New Mexico, ProQuest Dissertations Publishing, 2011.

Survivors of sexual violence and altruism: Designing a typology. Warner Stidham, Andrea. Kent State University, ProQuest Dissertations Publishing, 2009.

Survivors of sexual violence in Bosnia-Herzegovina and Kosovo (after the war in Yugoslavia) Skoric, Indira Kajosevic. Fielding Graduate University, ProQuest Dissertations Publishing, 2011.

Systematic sexual violence by U.S. State agencies: A victimology approach
Brightman, Sarah. Western Michigan University, ProQuest Dissertations Publishing, 2011.

Thinking about rape: The meaning of sexual violence for "non-victimized" women
Romani, Teresa. City University of New York, ProQuest Dissertations Publishing, 2002.

Vicarious traumatization and the role of supervision: An exploration of sexual violence counselors' stories. Sommer, Carol Ann. Southern Illinois University at Carbondale, ProQuest Dissertations Publishing, 2003.

Victims, heroes, survivors: Sexual violence on the Eastern Front during World War II
Gertjejanssen, Wendy Jo. University of Minnesota, ProQuest Dissertations Publishing, 2004.

Victims' voices: Sexual violence in the Armenian and Rwandan genocides. Bell, Kristin A.. Northeastern University, ProQuest Dissertations Publishing, 2015.

Violence involving sexual minorities in Japan. DiStefano, Anthony Salvatore. University of California, Los Angeles, ProQuest Dissertations Publishing, 2005.

Journal Articles about Sexual Violence

The Color of Violence: Violence against Women of Color. Andrea Smith. *Meridians*, Vol. 1, No. 2 (Spring, 2001), pp. 65-72.

Conflict, Power, and Violence in Families. Kristin L. Anderson. *Journal of Marriage and Family*, Vol. 72, No. 3 (June 2010), pp. 726-742.

Contextualizing Petro-Sexual Politics. Heather M. Turcotte. *Alternatives: Global, Local, Political*, Vol. 36, No. 3 (August 2011), pp. 200-220.

Domestic Violence and Symptoms of Gynecologic Morbidity among Women in North India. Rob Stephenson, Michael A. Koenig, Saifuddin Ahmed. *International Family Planning Perspectives*, Vol. 32, No. 4 (Dec., 2006), pp. 201-208.

Female Combatants and the Perpetration of Violence: Wartime Rape in the Sierra Leone Civil War. Dara Kay Cohen. *World Politics*, Vol. 65, No. 3 (July 2013), pp. 383-415.

Gender Empowerment and United Nations Peacebuilding. Gizelis, T-I. (2009). *Journal of Peace Research*, (46, 4). Pp. 505-523.

The Habitus of the Dominant: Addressing Rape and Sexual Assault at Rhodes University
Vivian de Klerk, Larissa Klazinga, Amy McNeill. Agenda: Empowering Women for Gender Equity, No. 74, *Rape: Gender Based Violence Trilogy*, 1,3 (2007), pp. 115-124.

Hidden violence is silent rape: sexual and gender-based violence in refugees, asylum seekers and undocumented migrants in Belgium and the Netherlands. Ines Keygnaert, Nicole Vettenburg, Marleen Temmerman. *Culture, Health & Sexuality*, Vol. 14, No. 5/6 (May-June 2012), pp. 505-520.

'I Just Wanted Him to Hear Me': Sexual Violence and the Possibilities of Restorative Justice
Clare McGlynn, Nicole Westmarland, Nikki Godden. *Journal of Law and Society*, Vol. 39, No. 2 (June 2012), pp. 213-240.

Imagined Violence/Queer Violence: Representation, Rage, and Resistance. Judith Halberstam. *Social Text*, No. 37, A Special Section Edited by Anne McClintock Explores the Sex Trade (Winter, 1993), pp. 187-201.

Intimate Partner Violence among Economically Disadvantaged Young Adult Women: Associations With Adolescent Risk-Taking and Pregnancy Experiences. Lydia O'Donnell, Gail Agronick, Richard Duran, Athi Myint-U, Ann Stueve. *Perspectives on Sexual and Reproductive Health*, Vol. 41, No. 2 (JUNE 2009), pp. 84-91.

Intimate Partner Violence and Anal Intercourse in Young Adult Heterosexual Relationships. Kristen L. Hess, Marjan Javanbakht, Joelle M. Brown, Robert E. Weiss, Paul Hsu, Pamina M. Gorbach. *Perspectives on Sexual and Reproductive Health*, Vol. 45, No. 1 (MARCH 2013), pp. 6-12.

Intimate Partner Violence and Increased Lifetime Risk of Sexually Transmitted Infection among Women in Ukraine. Annie Dude. *Studies in Family Planning*, Vol. 38, No. 2 (Jun., 2007), pp. 89-100.

A Model of Sexual Constraint and Sexual Emancipation. Andreas Schneider. *Sociological Perspectives*, Vol. 48, No. 2 (Summer 2005), pp. 255-270.

Not an Indian Tradition: The Sexual Colonization of Native Peoples. Andrea Smith. *Hypatia*, Vol. 18, No. 2, Indigenous Women in the Americas (Spring, 2003), pp. 70-85.

The Political Economy of the Cycles of Violence and Non-Violence in the Sikh Struggle for Identity and Political Power: Implications for Indian Federalism. Pritam Singh. *Third World Quarterly*, Vol. 28, No. 3 (2007), pp. 555-570.

Sex trafficking, sexual risk, sexually transmitted infection and reproductive health among female sex workers in Thailand. Michele R Decker, Heather L McCauley, Dusita Phuengsamran, Surang Janyam, Jay G Silverman. *Journal of Epidemiology and Community Health* (1979-), Vol. 65, No. 4 (April 2011), pp. 334-339.

Sexual Violence Prevention and Technologies of Gender among Heavy-Drinking College Women. Katherine P. Luke. *Social Service Review*, Vol. 83, No. 1 (March 2009), pp. 79-109.

Significant Silence in Elena Garro's Los perros. Jessica Burke. *Hispania*, Vol. 93, No. 1 (March 2010), pp. 23-28.

The silence of South-Sudanese women: social risks in talking about experiences of sexual violence Marian T.A. Tankink. *Culture, Health & Sexuality*, Vol. 15, No. 3/4 (March—April 2013), pp. 391-403.

Violence in Contract Work Among Female Sex Workers in Andhra Pradesh, India. Annie George, Shagun Sabarwal, P. Martin. *The Journal of Infectious Diseases*, Vol. 204, Supplement 5. Sex Work in Asia: Health, Agency, and Sexuality (1 December 2011), pp. s1235-s1240.

The Violence of Non-Violence: Law and War in Iraq. Samera Esmeir. *Journal of Law and Society*, Vol. 34, No. 1, Democracy's Empire: Sovereignty, Law, and Violence (Mar., 2007), pp. 99-115

Wartime Sexual Violence in Guatemala and Peru. Michele L. Leiby. *International Studies Quarterly*, Vol. 53, No. 2 (Jun., 2009), pp. 445-468.

Wartime Sexual Violence: Women's Human Rights and Questions of Masculinity. Miranda Alison. *Review of International Studies*, Vol. 33, No. 1 (Jan., 2007), pp. 75-90.

About the Editors

Dr. Stephanie Y. Evans is Professor and Chair of African American Studies, Africana Women's Studies, and History at Clark Atlanta University. She is author of *Anna Julia Cooper: Human Rights Educator* (Rowman & Littlefield, 2017); *Black Passports: Travel Memoirs as a Tool for Youth Empowerment* (SUNY, 2014); and *Black Women in the Ivory Tower, 1850-1954: An Intellectual History* (UF Press, 2007). Along with Purple Sparks, she is co-editor of several books including *African Americans and Community Engagement* (SUNY, 2010), and *Black Women's Mental Health: Balancing Strength and Vulnerability* (forthcoming).

She has taught Black studies, women's studies, and youth empowerment courses for almost two decades. In May 2003, Stephanie Evans received her Ph.D. in African American Studies with a concentration in History and Politics from the University of Massachusetts, Amherst and in May 2002 earned a Master's Degree in the same field. Also in 2002, she completed the Graduate Certificate Program in Advanced Feminist Studies. Dr. Evans's main research interest is Black women's intellectual and educational history in the United States. In her dissertation, Living Legacies: Black Women, Educational Philosophies, and Community Service, 1865-1965, she considered the educational ideas of four African American women educators: Fanny Jackson Coppin, Anna Julia Cooper, Mary McLeod Bethune, and Septima Clark. She has published foundational texts analyzing the past, present and future of graduate training in Africana Studies.

Dr. Evans is the creator of Purple Pens Poetry Workshops for Survivors of Sexual Violence. In addition to youthSpark, Dr. Evans has partnered with several non-profit agencies including Boys and Girls Clubs, Big Brothers/Big Sisters, and UNICEF. Her full profile is found online at www.professorevans.net.

Dr. Sharnell Myles Dr. Sharnell Myles, Psy. D., LPC is a licensed clinician who specializes in the treatment of complex trauma. Her dedication to serving children, youth, and adults has spanned over 16-years with a focus on utilizing trauma-informed services to treat sexual abuse, physical abuse, domestic minor sex trafficking, and community based trauma. Dr. Myles is the CEO/Owner of JoyUs Beginnings Child & Family Wellness Center and The Urban Trauma: Positive Impact Center which is an exclusive trauma-informed treatment and advocacy agency located in Atlanta, Georgia. She is also the Care Clinician and Voices Facilitator for youthSpark, Inc. a non-profit agency located at the Fulton County Juvenile Court. youthSpark, Inc. is dedicated to eradicating domestic minor sex trafficking through prevention and research. Voices is youthSpark's signature direct service prevention program and provides psychoeducation, case management, and advocacy to youth with high risk behaviors increasing their vulnerability to trafficking.

Dr. Myles has been deemed an expert in legal cases involving child and adolescent trauma. She currently serves as the Chair of the DeKalb County Juvenile Court Journey Program and the Vice Chair of the Georgia Statewide Human Trafficking Taskforce Workgroup 7 - Survivors Supported and Protected. JoyUs Beginnings is also a partner agency with the State of Georgia Criminal Justice Coordinating Council Human Trafficking Taskforce and a member of the Georgia Statewide Multidisciplinary Team for DMST. She has presented as various conferences and has experience in vast settings such as clinical, juvenile justice, military, and community-based settings. Dr. Myles is a teacher at heart and by trade. She provides clinical supervision to "budding" therapists and consultation services and trainings to various disciplines.

Dr. Myles has a Bachelor in psychology and Master's degree in Community and Clinical Psychology from Norfolk State University. She also has a Master's degree and a Doctor of

Psychology degree (child/adolescent and assessment concentration) from Georgia School of Professional Psychology at Argosy University in Atlanta, Georgia.
For more information, visit www.joyusbeginnings.com.

Jennifer Swain presently works as the Deputy Director for youthSpark, Inc. (formerly the Juvenile Justice Fund) where she oversees the strategic implementation of current programs and community education initiatives as well as manages other internal activities of the organization. Prior to the current position, Jennifer served as the Program Director where her influential vision aided in the development of youthSpark Voices, the unique early intervention program to reach girls deemed high-risk for trafficking involvement or who do not self-identify as victims of commercial sexual exploitation.

She speaks and trains various groups on the trafficking issue, as well as presenting at various local and national conferences on victim identification and early intervention. She has worked as a consultant with groups working to build community collaborations and strategies to address this problem. She is a part of the Georgia Statewide Trafficking Task Force and the National Center for Missing & Exploited Children Family Advocacy & Outreach Network, a network of providers and agencies who help to link trafficking victims and their families to services and support when needed in Georgia. Additionally, Swain served as a trainer for Georgia Attorney General Sam Olens' Georgia's Not Buying It Campaign and has been declared an expert testimony witness by DeKalb County Superior Court.

Prior to her work in the non-profit world, Swain worked in programming and communications for FOX5/WZDX in Alabama and has experience working with youth through mentorship and her longtime volunteer work with Big Brothers Big Sisters. She is a graduate of Alabama A&M University with a Bachelor of Arts Degree in Communications with countless hours of specialized trafficking training & education from various federal and local agencies.